SURVIVING THE START-UP YEARS

SURVIVING THE START-UP YEARS

in your own business

Joyce S. Marder

BETTERWAY PUBLICATIONS, INC.
WHITE HALL, VIRGINIA

Published by Betterway Publications, Inc.
P.O. Box 219
Crozet, VA 22932
(804) 823-5661

Cover design by Rick Britton
Typography by Kurt H. Fischer

Library of Congress Cataloging-in-Publication Data

Marder, Joyce S.
  Surviving the start-up years in your own business / Joyce S. Marder.
  p. cm.
  Includes index.
  ISBN 1-55870-200-8 (pbk.) : $7.95
  1. New business enterprises—United States. I. Title.
    HD62.5.M356 1991
  658.1'141—dc20   91-17993
                                                            CIP

Printed in the United States of America
0 9 8 7 6 5 4 3 2 1

To Budd Lee Bingham
for his personal support and love
and
the members of the League of Utah Writers for their professional
guidance and encouragement.

This book is also dedicated to all those people who have granted
me the time to interview them, or who have simply told me their
stories because they were my customers and we had something in
common to talk about.

Acknowledgments

Some of the quoted material in this book first appeared in *City Center Magazine*, Salt Lake City, Utah.

Contents

1

A GOOD IDEA MAY OR MAY NOT BE A GOOD BUSINESS

There are lots of reasons to start your own business. My reason was that my employer offered me the opportunity. He asked if I wanted to form a partnership with him and turn the typesetting department of his quick-print shop into a separate business.

My father had always preached self-employment, even though he was a well-paid corporate executive. "You'll never get rich working for someone else," I remember him saying. At one time he thought about going into business for himself. But he had to pay for the lifestyle to which he and his wife had grown accustomed. So he remained a loyal corporate employee. Since I don't remember my father ever saying much more than that, I suppose it took on some internal importance to me. When the opportunity arose, I took the risk.

Whatever the reason, and I have heard many, the only real reason anyone should go into business is to make money. Nothing else counts — not ego satisfaction, not making a difference in the world, not the joy of running your own show — because when there is no income derived from your hard work, all the other reasons go away. The jobs you create for your loyal employees, the satisfaction you derive from a job well done, are byproducts of running a profitable business.

WHAT IS A PROFITABLE BUSINESS?

What is a "profitable" business? At the very minimum it is one that pays its bills, in cash, and affords the owner a decent standard of living. We're not talking yachts, Park Avenue penthouses, and six month cruises around the world. We're talking about food, clothing, shelter, monthly entertainment, and enough income so that you never have to look over your shoulder in fear of bill collectors. Enough income so you (and your family, if applicable) can sleep nights and look forward to what each day brings.

How much is enough? Later I will talk about salaries in detail. But for the owner, "enough" depends on your age, your debts, your expectations, and where you live. Twenty thousand dollars buys a lot in Salt Lake City,

Utah, where many of the entrepreneurs profiled in this book conduct business. In New York City, you would have to have a small apartment and a lot of roommates on that income.

How Much Will You Need to Make?

If you are between eighteen and twenty-five years of age, and "just starting out," a small apartment, a stocked refrigerator, a weekly trip to a fast food joint with a date, and money left over for an occasional movie is probably "enough." If you are twenty-five to thirty-five and have worked for a number of years, you have probably acquired some furniture and an automobile. Perhaps you are a couple and have incurred new expenses, like a house payment, child care, or medical care. You will need more money to "get by." Once you reach thirty-six (my age when I wrote this book) and realize that you have about thirty years left to prepare for retirement, you will want to afford all of the above, plus a plushy annual vacation, and to save and invest a bunch of money for retirement. In Salt Lake City (where I now live) that's at least $30,000 a year without kids and $40-50,000 a year with kids (1991 dollars). In New York City (where my brother lives) it's about $80,000. (He's close; I'm not. He has never been self-employed; I have.)

Deduct from that salary figure your estimated value of "amenities." Is managing your own time, working your own hours, taking Monday off, having a no-smoking office worth something to you? Probably. Put a dollar amount on that and subtract it from what you feel you must earn. You will pay a price when you are self-employed: insecurity, long hours, high Social Security taxes. Put a dollar amount on those too, and decide how much you must earn to make it worth your while to be in business for yourself. Then set a deadline by which you expect to earn that amount. It is unlikely that you will earn what you want — what you are worth — soon. Starting a new business requires an investment in both money and time. No formula exists to help you know how long it will take to earn what you want, if your business succeeds. But you can take an educated guess.

This educated guess is part of the research you should do before you start your business. Now that you have decided what you are worth, it's time to take a look at the product or service you intend to sell to the public. You must determine if it has a value. You must find out if people are willing to buy what you want to sell, and if you can make money selling it for that price.

RESEARCH

Business textbooks contain a lot of information about how to do market research. Basically, you should survey people and find out if they want a product or service, how often they will use it, what they are willing to pay, how far they will travel to obtain it, etc. The problem with that type of formal research is twofold: 1) people don't know what they want or how much they are willing to pay for something *when* you survey them; and 2) it is very expensive to do this type of research. Large companies with large research and development budgets do it all the time; it doesn't always work.

Small businesses rarely do survey research. Something else happens that takes the place of a formal study and produces the same, if not more accurate, information. This is experience. Of the twenty people I've interviewed (for published magazine articles) who started new businesses, three started based on a hobby, four turned a part-time avocation into a full-time career and business, one stumbled upon the idea and made it work, and eleven (including myself) worked for someone else in the same or a similar line of work. Among those businesses, four employ two generations (including the business I have since sold).

Why do so many people turn a job into self-employment? The best reason is that they have something upon which to base a decision. By working for someone else, you are, in a way, doing market research. You can see if people come into your employer's place of business, what they buy, how much they spend. And, most important, you can hear what they complain about. Then you can decide if you can do it better and make money doing it.

A Few Case Histories

Guy Lester, owner of The Ringmaker, a custom jewelry shop, worked as a manager for Heritage Keepsake Diamonds. When the company he worked for declared bankruptcy (Chapter 11) and later sold out, he was offered a new position with the takeover company. Guy says that prompted him to start his own company. He decided he could do a better job for himself. He and a partner started in a 100-year-old house as jewelry manufacturers. When a retail location became available in a new section of a mall downtown, Lester and partner Paul Chapman obtained a loan from the eleventh bank they tried. When the money ran out, the pair spent nights in sleeping bags on the floor of their new store to make an inventory.

What did he do differently than the original business? Guy specialized in custom-made jewelry and only had one store. John Felt, the original owner of Keepsake, had a large inventory of manufactured pieces, purchased with bank loans at high interest rates. Furthermore, "investors" had induced him into opening fifteen stores based on the success of his first. When John asked for the cash the investors had promised, he discovered that the only investment they had ever planned to make was advice (which is usually the case).

Rhett Barney, owner of Frankly My Dear, a designer-label women's clothing resale shop, worked for a similar business. He sold women's clothing for fifteen years before he opened his own business. He knew his market well and noticed that women who buy better dresses tend to buy new items frequently. He concluded that a lot of fine merchandise was hanging in closets. So, when he started, he called his former customers (he had kept a list over the years as do most professional retail salespeople) and asked them if they would like to sell their "old" dresses on consignment. "I went to some of their homes," he says, "others brought things to me: garbage bags full. As the word spread at social functions and bridge clubs, it snowballed." Most of his inventory was less than six months old. He also added market samples to his line, and he carried accessories, both used items and those produced by local designers.

Barney also put his experience in visual display to use in his own business. Unlike most resale shops where customers have to push garments along bars and dig for bargains, Barney artfully draped Ralph Lauren, Charles Jourdan, Halston Ultrasuede, and Argenti dresses over chairs and displayed slacks, shirts, and skirts on clothing stands. He said a willingness to put in long hours overcame an initial lack of capital.

Judy Harris, owner of Classy Lady, a women's fashion store, worked for a similar women's shop that closed. When her employer quit, Judy's husband suggested that she start her own business. The lease on the mall space where she had worked was available. So she took the risk. Only two-thirds of the inventory she ordered that September for Christmas sales actually arrived. But she says her first season was "OK. I had the advantage that this was a clothing store before, and since it's in a mall location, people just stumbled in." Five years later, she had two mall stores. Her clothing is high fashion, and her prices are directed toward the medium income woman. She attributes her success to one-on-one service, something she learned from her former employer, she says, and repeat business. Judy says her most successful salespeople help their customers find pieces that coordinate with previous years' purchases. She has built her business on the concept that today's women are interested in "investment dressing."

Judy, Rhett, and Guy did the easiest and cheapest type of market research. They simply learned by doing. None of them set out to be self-employed. But they gained certain skills and used their intelligence to recognize what their employers were doing to make money — and what more they could do. They had access to other information that encouraged them to go off on their own. They knew how much inventory costs, appropriate markups for their industries, where and how to promote their businesses, how and from whom to buy supplies or merchandise. They knew for a fact that some people would buy that type of product at certain prices. There were also a lot of things they could not know until they tried it for themselves, which is what this book is about. Still, what these three people did was to take a calculated risk.

My experience is similar. I worked for the owner of a quick-print shop as a typesetter. I had a little background in layout and pasteup and using IBM machines. My employer taught me how to use the IBM Composer (you can find one in a museum or the trade-in department of IBM), and six months later he said he thought it would be a good idea if the typesetting service became a separate business so that it could attract work from other small printing businesses. I had the numbers (monthly income and expenses). As part of my job, I kept track of time and billing. I knew that the typesetting "business," with my partner's two print shops as its only customers, would generate an income I could live on. In fact, I would get an automatic $100 raise. That raise would cost me a $7,000 investment—half of our estimated value of the company's assets. I would be paid back in the first year, doing the same work I was already doing. Essentially, I was willing to work for free for less than one year to have part ownership in a business.

There are other, more risky ways to start a business. For instance, if you have a hobby you are particularly adept at and your friends buy what you make, you might want to start a business based on that. Proceed slowly. Before you quit your job, try it part-time. When your avocation is producing as much income as your full-time job, then quit your job and build your business. While friends may want to buy your handicrafts or photographs, that does not necessarily mean that the general public will — that you can make a living off it. Remember, when you sell a hobby, you sell your own time, and there are only twenty-four hours in a day. Your income is limited by the number of items you can produce and the hourly rate you charge for each piece. For example, a strip of tatted lace takes me three days of bus rides to produce. I don't think anyone would pay the $5.00 I might charge to justify my time. (That's $5.00 an hour.) After all, wages are lower in the Far East, so how could I compete? The trick is to sell someone else's time.

Marie Cavanaugh started making chocolates for Christmas gifts. Then she taught the women at her church how to dip chocolates to sell at church fundraisers. The project was so successful, she and her husband George spend much of their time traveling to neighboring towns in South Dakota to market their products. Neighboring towns were between 50 and 225 miles away! So, they moved their family to Bountiful, Utah and opened a candy factory and retail store in 1972. By 1987, the company employed seventy-three full- and part-time employees and had four company-owned stores and four department store outlets. Marie and George Cavanaugh did the best kind of research. They sold the candy they produced to a lot of people and made money. They knew they could hire other people and pay a good wage, and still sell their chocolates for a profit. The Cavanaughs left a 1,000-acre ranch because the chocolate business held a more promising future.

Carrie Bissell's experience is similar. A flight attendant at the time, Carrie had a strong interest in aerobics. She didn't just "do" aerobic exercises, she studied physiology and came to understand muscles and how they work and what types of movement are useful for the development of which muscles. At first, her interest was strictly personal. Then she decided to give classes when she had the time. With just a classified ad and answering machine attached to her home telephone, she attracted students to her basement aerobics classes. As the aerobics movement caught on and demand went up, Carrie made the move to a studio, but kept her flying job so she could afford to pay the rent no matter what happened. Her message machine continued to fill classes. Eventually, she began to take leaves of absence to teach twelve to fifteen classes a week in advanced aerobics. When flight delays made it impossible to get back to Salt Lake for the classes, Carrie had to make a career decision. She followed demand and by 1987 employed sixteen instructors who teach beginning, intermediate, and advanced aerobics. Carrie still teaches, but since she is selling someone else's time, she has been able to devote more of her own talent and energy to video production and personalized instruction. By the time Carrie made the move from hobby to business, she knew that people, lots of people, were willing to pay money to learn what she had to teach. She expanded and finally created a successful business by finding other people who could also teach. They make a good salary, and she makes a handsome income.

Going into the family business is the best head start anyone could ever hope for; most offspring resist the idea. It must be human nature (in America) to prove that "one can make it on one's own." Afterward, the children come back to work in the family business. What better source of information could anyone ask for than the help, guidance, advice, and financial backing of one's own parents. Robert Hale manages one of his parents' five Hallmark card shops. Merlyn Neff Olson manages her parents' floral business. Her grandmother Retta sold flowers from her garden in the 1930s. Mike Mihlberger drew on his experience working for his father's retail typewriter company to start his own office supply business, after six years of working an assortment of jobs not related to office products, attending college, and traveling the world. Unlike his father's business, Mike's Office & Things carries an assortment of both practical and whimsical office equipment and accessories.

I've only interviewed one (successful) business owner in the past two years who ended up in business by accident. Charlie Hastings' father-in-law bought a roll-top desk and asked Charlie to take it apart and figure out how it was made. The attempt was futile, but the timing was perfect. The man who had sold the roll-top wanted to sell his business. Hastings was a sheet metal worker by trade. Luckily, the company came with a loyal employee who knew the art of roll-top desk construction, and Charlie was in business. He did learn the art. One can speculate that his ability to work with his hands enabled him to learn another craft. But running a business was foreign to Charlie. Competition from Taiwan made him change his product, for a short time, to veneer-top models. Not happy with what he was doing, Charlie went back to producing only solid oak desks and marketing them to business people who can afford custom-made, quality furniture. Wood Revival Furniture now has more demand than it can fill. A custom designed, one-of-a-kind roll-top desk costs $6,000 and may take up to three months to complete.

Charlie's business is limited by time. There are only so many desks he can make if each one takes three months to produce. Furthermore, it will not be as easy for Charlie to sell someone else's time as it is for Marie Cavanaugh or Mike Mihlberger. Not many people have the talent, patience, or willingness to learn to make roll-top desks. It's hard, messy, and somewhat hazardous work. Candy dipping and clerking in an office supply store are easier to learn, the supply of available labor is ample, and the amount of money this type of worker will expect to earn is lower. Wood Revival Furniture is successful, according to the definition at the beginning of this chapter. But Mike and Marie have a better chance of getting rich. Still, who's to say that's important? Guy falls somewhere in between; he also makes much of his own product. But he has been able to attract people who have learned jewelry making. The time involved in making a ring is days, not months. The available pool of willing and capable labor is ample.

IF YOU CAN'T MAKE A PROFIT ...

Which leads to the conclusion of this chapter: *If it won't sell profitably, forget it.* Maybe you can sell your tatted lace trim to friends, but you won't sell enough to make a living. If you have to pay $1,000 an ounce for gold, and the public is only willing to pay $900 for that ounce turned into a handcrafted work of art, you are going to lose money. Or, as happened to me, if your technology becomes outdated, it's time to change your product or get out of business, or never start it. For Charlie, foreign competition determined that American-made veneer top desks (produced at American wages) would not sell. We live in a world economy to a great extent. Keep that in mind when you are deciding what business to start. While Marie's hand-dipped chocolate is less expensive than most imported chocolate, lots of products and services can be manufactured overseas for less. So if you think you have a wonderful idea because no one else in your town is doing it, look again. Maybe lots of others were doing it and went out of business because of foreign competition. Or, if they were smart, they did the "research" you should do (or learn from) and determined that they could not compete with foreign-made goods, and never started at all.

How about those one-of-a-kind ideas like the pet rock, Cabbage Patch dolls, and Frisbees? If you come up with one of those, you'll just have to believe in yourself and the willingness of the American public to spend money on frivolous, fun, or unique ideas. Do it first, do it fast, make your million; and when imports start to resemble your product, move on to the next brilliant idea. Of the above, Frisbees are the only one that has lasted over time. The others were fads. People can get rich off of fads. But the person who markets, distributes, and promotes will make the money — not necessarily the person who did the inventing. What good does a pet rock do you if you only sell it to people in your own town? You have to get it in every gift shop in the land, all at once, and advertise it. Just look at the track record.

Some people go into business because they have always wanted to. They sell things they know nothing about; they have no idea if anyone will buy what they are trying to sell. Their prices are too high, more often too low. They lose interest quickly because they expected it to be easy; it never is. Starting a business is like writing a good article: you have to be interested; you have to know your subject; and you have to be able to communicate that knowledge and interest to other people. Keep that in mind as you examine yourself and your interests, hobbies, vocation, and avocation for the business you should start.

2

MONEY AND MANAGEMENT

You can start a business with very little capital. But expect to spend at least the first two to five years trying to overcome this disadvantage. The reason a small business needs capital is that there is a need to spend money before you earn it. In retail, you have to have an inventory to sell. No matter how far back in the manufacturing-distribution-wholesale-retail-service chain you go, you still need supplies. Guy, The Ringmaker, must purchase gold; Charlie, Wood Revival, needs wood. The only business I can think of that has almost no start-up cost is panning for gold. All you need is a pan. But gold panners also make no money until they find gold dust in the stream. Even the timber operation that supplies Charlie with his wood has had to invest in expensive equipment, hire expensive labor, and plant new trees for the ones cut down — so there will be something to harvest in the future.

CAPITAL AND CASH FLOW

Managing capital and cash flow is even more complex for service businesses. In quick printing, typesetting, and publishing, all of which I have experience doing, the customer receives the product or service and pays upon receipt, or over time. The difference is, in retail the owner invests capital in an inventory that can stay in the store until someone pays to take it home. With service, the owner must invest not only capital to purchase supplies, but time and labor to produce the end product. If the customer is not satisfied, or bounces a check, the loss is much greater. You cannot unmake a magazine or brochure because someone decided not to pay you. You can't put business cards back on the shelf for someone else to buy. Unlike a couch or a camera, it makes no sense, nor will it generate any future income, if you repossess business stationery. The loss is total. You can't take ink off paper, or uncut business cards. And you can't get your time back and use it to produce a product for a paying customer.

That is why you need capital. It will come from somewhere. Business owners who start with very little money can create working capital by forgoing a salary. If the business you start generates enough cash for you to take home a salary, and you choose not to, in effect you are investing capital in your business. This sounds obvious. But too many businesses are started by people who want to get rich quick. They take home more cash than their businesses can support. They go broke.

Since you need a product to sell, either in the form of goods on the shelf of a retail store, or the cost of producing a service or product, you need money to cover those expenses. I had a camera in my typesetting business that photographically reproduced black and white artwork for printing — a "stat camera." I bought boxes of film for $100 per 100 sheets. By the time the box was used up, I had made a handsome "profit" on the film, but I had to spend some of that profit to buy the next box, as well as pay rent, phone, and service bills. If I sold a lot of film (in the form of stats or PMTs) coupled with my other services, I generated sufficient cash flow to keep myself in supplies as well as take home a paycheck.

So it goes. If you publish a magazine, you have to pay photographers, typesetters, printers, perhaps a mailing service. It doesn't matter if those people are subcontractors or are on your payroll, those are your expenses. If your customers pay over time, you will have half of your money when the contract to place an ad is signed and half after the magazine is printed and distributed. But you still have all those costs of doing business, whether or not you are able to collect all those receivables.

DON'T RUN YOUR BUSINESS ON CREDIT

The reason many businesses get into trouble is their suppliers let them. Credit is the way Americans buy things. It is also the way many businesses try to stay in business. I felt too nervous asking my suppliers to wait more than the thirty days they agreed to wait for their money. At times I went without a paycheck for thirty days so I could keep my bills current. But my debts were relatively small — always less than my actual monthly income. That means I was running a successful business.

But if you are starting from scratch, trying to build a clientele, you will probably spend more money up front than you take in. Perhaps your suppliers will let you stretch your debts for more than thirty days. That's fine as long as you can make the payments. But watch out the first time you are late. Your suppliers are not in business to be your banker, anymore than you, as a start-up company, want to be a banker for your customers. They need cash, too, to pay their suppliers, their employees, and themselves. Eventually, they will ask you to "pay up" and if you are still taking in less cash than it is costing you to produce your product or service, you will begin to spend most of your time talking to lawyers instead of clients. Two rules govern working capital:

1. Good management can overcome a lack of start-up capital.

2. Capital can never overcome a lack of good management.

Why? Simple: If you are a good manager, you will know when you can and cannot afford to pay yourself. You will know when too much debt threatens your business, and you will make the necessary changes to get out of debt by selling more or producing less or increasing productivity. You will only make promises you can keep, and you will stay honest. If you are a good manager, given enough time (and it may take years) you will find a way to generate a cash flow that will pay the bills, and you will make your business work — assuming your business is based on "research" and you are in a viable business. Finally, if you are a good manager, and you remain honest and keep payments current, opportunities will open for you. Banks will consider making you loans; investors may find your company an attractive risk. That's because they will believe that you are in business for the long haul, because you have the ability to make the company succeed.

MONEY MANAGEMENT

On the other hand, if you are not a good manager, throwing money into the company will only hasten its demise. Poor managers tend to be shortsighted. They want their boats and cars now. They don't make choices based on the bottom line (income, expenses, and profits). They react to problems out of desperation, rather than calmly handling each situation. And when things get really bad, they lie and they hide. They're never around to answer the phone when a supplier calls to collect money. They're never around to answer their employees' questions. They get greedy, forget promises, and start to act as though they're doing everyone a big favor by providing jobs. They let their emotions take over their brains and start to make bad choice after bad choice. They start to ask people to invest money, and they spend so much time looking for investors to bail them out that they forget to do their job. Bad managers don't sell anymore, or manage. They "don't have the time."

Banks and investors loan money to make money, not to save you. They are not interested in bailing you out. They are interested in putting their money to work so that it generates interest, dividends, or capital gains. If you are going to throw their capital at old bills, then this probably won't happen. When you use their capital to buy supplies or equipment you will use to produce more or better products or services, that you can sell to generate more profits, this becomes an "investment."

LENDERS AND INVESTORS

Don't look for someone to save you. Don't confuse lenders with investors. Lenders demand a fixed return on their money over a fixed period of time. Investors do not. Still, investors will invest if they can expect a return on their money at some future time. If you need money to pay debts, sell your house, your car, your boat first; put that money to work in your business. Turn it around, then look for investors.

While investors cannot demand repayment like lenders, they will ask for something even more vital to your business — control. Investors are interested in future dividends and capital gains, which they expect will be higher than the interest you would pay a lender. Furthermore, they will want some control over their investment, which means control over your new business. If you are asking for a lot of money, expect to give up a lot of control. This can work to your advantage or disadvantage. If you are a good manager, you don't need or want the interference. If you are not, and you pick an investor who has a proven track record of successfully running small companies, maybe it's time to relinquish control so that your business can turn around and become more profitable. Base your decision on how well you know yourself and how much you want to trust a stranger. But if you have sold everything you own to keep your business afloat, a clearer head might not be a bad idea. Just remember to check the potential investor's background as carefully as he or she has checked yours. And put everything in writing. Even if your investor is a close friend or relative, it is best to write down your mutual expectations, responsibilities, and obligations.

RAISING CAPITAL

How do you raise capital? Look to yourself first. Even if you do get a bank loan, you're more likely to find a banker who will lend you money if you believe in yourself and your business idea enough to spend your own money. Perhaps you have some cash saved, or have come into an inheritance.

I hear lots of people say, "But I can't spend that money. I have to save it for retirement." True; but what did you plan to do with that money between now and when you retire? Invest it, I hope. If you're the type to stuff money in a mattress, you're not the type to run a small business. If you would buy stocks or mutual funds, isn't that taking a risk on someone else's management ability? You bet it is! Why not take the same (perhaps less) risk on your own ability to manage.

Professional money managers examine a company's product, income pattern, and management ability. You should invest in yourself in the same way. That's why so many of the business people I have interviewed based their businesses on their own professional background. They recognized their own skill, and felt they could do at least as well as their former employers. Their former employers paid their salaries; so those businesses had to do at least well enough to meet payroll (which must be paid first; bills are second, but a close second), just to keep the doors open.

But, you say, you've always spent everything you've ever earned. You're young and just starting out and have never made an income to save. Bankers won't even talk with you. There are other ways. Look first to relatives — mothers and fathers, for example. Just tell them you want to take a chance; show them the same facts and figures you would show a banker. Put in writing that the money is a gift, not an investment or a partnership interest (unless you all agree to do it that way). Then use that money to keep yourself and your business alive while you build your cash flow.

Friends may invest in your business. This gets complicated. If you use this source for capital, make certain your friends understand they are taking a risk, there are no guarantees, and they don't get to run your company.

Sources of Capital

The government (Small Business Administration) and venture capitalists can provide additional sources of capital. The first requires that two banks turn you down, then the government may guarantee the loan. In rare instances the government actually makes the loan. Government funds are scarce these days. SBA loans require lots of time and paperwork. I know one person who has used that source. He says he thinks he qualified because of his medical disability. Venture capitalists may invest in your business, but they will want some say-so in how your company is run.

PARTNERSHIPS

Starting a business with a partner can work well, especially if one person has management ability and professional expertise and the other has capital. But, as in any "marriage," people change. Just make certain that you both (all) agree upon the nature of your business, your individual responsibilities, your goals, and even how to end the partnership. Each partner should write out his or her expectations prior to starting the company. Compare notes, reach an agreement, then put your "Partnership Agreement" in writing and *sign* it. Paragraph one should begin: "Why we are going into business together." Have a statement of purpose; you may need a reminder as time passes. Also write down which assets belong to the company and what is on loan from individuals. Write down how much each of you will be paid and when; what percentage of profits each will take home and when. Define "profits."

Do you need a lawyer for this? Yes and no. My partner and I wrote our own contract and took it to a lawyer who retyped it and added a few "parties of the first part, hereinafter referred to as ...'s. Still, our willingness to have a lawyer look at our contract made us both more comfortable. We had only known each other for six months and he had been my boss.

Getting out is easier. If one of you changes your mind, you should have a clause in your original agreement that states how to dissolve the partnership. The end of a partnership may or may not enable one partner to remain in the same business. Say, for instance, you all agreed to buy each other out for a certain sum of money. But when the time arises, the partner obliged to do the buying does not want to pay that price. You can try to renegotiate. Or you can just close down. Go your separate ways, take out a new business license, and with all that you have learned and saved, start over on your own.

What if one partner just stops participating in the business? Say he or she has started taking a lot of long vacations, or just never shows up to work, as agreed upon in the partnership agreement. This happened to me. For about a year, my partner, Fred, was never around when I needed his help. I ran Midnight Oil Typesetting on my own; his half of our deal was to run his print shops so as to generate business for our typesetting company. He got into financial trouble and started to be "invisible," figuratively speaking. Business was dropping off and I resented my obligation to give him 51% of the profits, since he wasn't putting forth his agreed-upon 51% of the effort.

He took half of the equipment and I took half. He was a reasonable man and left me with the right half to enable me to continue doing business. Shortly thereafter, I invested another $2,000 into the company to buy a "stat" camera. I would not have made that investment in "our" company.

While his print shops remained in business, the new owner made little effort to market typesetting. My customer base quickly eroded, and I had to work hard to replace it with new business. That wasn't the way we had planned it; it's the way things went. I managed to keep the doors open, provide the service, and take home the same salary (but not more) for two and a half more years.

It could have been worse. Guy's partner died in a car accident. Afterward, Guy chose to remain in business, twice moving to better locations in the mall. I ran into a former business associate who told me her partner just got tired of living in Salt Lake and moved to California. She insisted that her partners buy her out at the price she set. They closed the business instead.

But the saddest situation I know, firsthand, is when someone assumed she was a partner when she was not. In gratitude for Molly's help in launching her company, Edna (not her real name) gave Molly stock in her corporation and the title of secretary/treasurer on the incorporation papers. The problem was that they never agreed to be "partners." There was nothing in writing that promised Molly an equal share of management say-so or a percentage of profits. Since the financial investment was primarily Edna's and her husband's, Molly was powerless to insist on any proprietary interest.

Things worked out fine when the business was new, enthusiasm was high, and the bottom line was in (or near) the black. But when Edna began to sell ads on trade, she kept all the goods. She also complained that she wasn't "getting paid," since she "took no cash home." The staff (including myself) had little sympathy for that type of thinking. Edna's responsibility was to sell and manage; Molly's was bidding and art direction, according to their verbal agreement. At first, they consulted and agreed before taking on new projects or spending capital. Then Edna just took off on her own, and Molly heard the news later. Eventually, Molly's input into the affairs of the company was less than nothing. Any advice or counsel she offered was ignored or fought. And since nothing was in writing, she was powerless to protest. Eventually, Molly took employment elsewhere.

DEALING WITH FINANCIAL TROUBLE

I have seen financial problems change people: my partner, my employers, close friends. More often than not, people who are in financial trouble do two things predictably: they lie and they hide. You will be able to discover both. They won't be around to manage their businesses on a day-to-day basis, which is vital to any new company. They just run in once a week in a panic to find out what needs fixing that day. Then, unable to pay the bills or stand the pressure, they disappear. They also lie. They start to say there's enough money in the bank, when the daily mail proves differently. They start to say that the store will have 100 bicycle parts delivered Friday; Friday comes and goes and the parts don't show. They make excuses, like the truck was delayed. And when some parts arrive and you count the boxes, there are only fifty. As happened to me, the owner will either explain it away: "It just isn't cost-effective to only send bike parts without any bikes," when your storage room is ceiling high in bikes; or will call the supplier and rant and rave. You may see a lot of flailing arms and hear angry tones. But the other fifty parts will never show up. Meanwhile, you have promised your customers their bicycles would be repaired a week after you anticipated the shipment. You have become a part of the lie. I left two jobs because someone made me part of the lie.

You cannot fix another person's integrity. If your business partner starts to manifest these symptoms, get out. If your employer does, that's a good time to launch your own business. Because if there is money to be made, but bad management has simply alienated suppliers and clients, then you have a good piece of information upon which to base a better business. Just make certain that management is the problem, not increased competition or outdated technology or a major change in consumer demand. These things get people into financial trouble, too, and the symptoms are the same. If you plan to compete with your former employer and use some of the same suppliers, start with enough capital to pay cash for a year or two. Those suppliers are probably trying to collect a pile of receivables and may be wary of a similar new operation. Build confidence and a line of credit by paying cash for a time.

If technological changes are the root of the problem, and you can afford the state-of-the-art equipment that will give you a marketing lead, try it. AlphaGraphics has always done business this way. When my partner was still making payments on his IBM copy machine, which produced gray, wrinkled copies, AlphaGraphics entered the marketplace with the top-of-the-line Xerox® machine, and the owner has continued to upgrade his equipment every time the photocopy machine manufacturers make a major product improvement. When competitors entered the field with machines that also copied, collated, and stapled, AlphaGraphics branched off into do-it-yourself desktop publishing. The company is seldom alone in the marketplace for long, but tends to be first with machinery and marketing.

PLANNING FOR THE FUTURE

Which brings up the last point about capital. You must have some money in the bank to pay your bills, but you also need to save some of your profits, over time, so that you will be able to improve your business as times change. Tastes also change, and your large inventory of handwoven baskets may suddenly start to collect dust after years of brisk sales. You must have enough savings so you can sell those baskets at a loss just to free up shelf space, plus money to buy whatever is in demand at the moment. Of course, you can always cut back your own salary or spend personal savings to update your business. But your goal should be for your business to become self-sustaining. The income and profits that your business generates should pay for both supplies and capital improvements. If you are always dipping into your personal bank account to pay business expenses, your business is either unsuccessful or you have taken too much out in salary in the first place.

If you are in the service business (or manufacturing) and use computers or any type of machinery, you should anticipate the day when someone will invent a machine that does more, works faster, and costs less to operate than what you are using now. This happened to Fred's print shop. It also happened to my typesetting business. Fred spent money on a third location, which attracted almost no business. He ended up in debt, but found a buyer for his business-in-trouble. It took four more years for the business to close.

I realized that desktop publishing was enabling businesses to do the same thing I was selling but cheaper and faster. I realized that the "low end" of the typesetting business was changing. The demand for typesetting was going to require phototypesetting equipment, which meant a $20-40,000 investment and employees to keep those machines working all day (and night) to justify that investment. I decided to sell my business. I admit to some sort of luck. A customer of mine who had a high-paying state job asked me if I wanted a partner. Bev Miller said she and her husband could use the tax deductions and her eighteen-year-old daughter, who had shown some interest in graphic arts, needed a job. Bev was also interested in retiring from her state job and moving into a business of her own.

I told her my view of the future; she agreed and rather than buying a partnership agreed to buy the entire business. Four years later, the company employed three daughters and Bev. Each of the daughters earns more than I ever did. But they have also invested tens of thousands of dollars in the business and are in for the long term. It might be another year or five before they recover their investment. But they bought the technology with which to do it. And while I had very little to do with it, people I meet who still do business there often say, "You started Midnight Oil Typesetting!" They must wonder how I could leave something so successful. Well, it was always successful, but it is a different business now. They typeset for five print shops and accept jobs that my machinery could never have handled. Any regrets on my part? None. I didn't want to be a typesetter forever; I wanted to write. As a writer, I earn less; but I like myself better, which is important too.

So before you get started in a small business, it would be wise to decide if you want to be in that line of work for a long time. Some people start businesses just to get them started, then they sell them to people who want to be in that line of work for a lifetime. Such people have sufficient capital to launch a new business quickly and try to sell it. They are willing to accept both success and failure; when they fail they dust themselves off and try again. Some of these people are crooks and are selling promises, not businesses.

For anyone who is considering starting his or her own business, know that costs are high at first and income is relatively low. Are you willing to stick with it? Other factors cause costs to be high and profits low as well. These reasons relate to capital and cash flow. When you start a new company, no one wants to give you credit. They want cash. They want to get their money before you get yours. As time goes by, your ability to pay suppliers after you have sold the products you made with those supplies increases. You don't have to use your own money or the company's start-up capital. You can now pay bills with income or working capital.

ADVERTISING AND CASH FLOW

Another reason cash flow is slow at first is that it will take time before people know your business exists, and more time until lots of them buy what you are selling. You can shorten this start-up time by advertising and promoting your business before you open the doors. Market Street Grill restaurant had local residents anticipating its opening with billboards that read: "Fresh Seafood." A bold statement and bright graphic caught freeway commuters' attention months before the words: "Market Street Grill" were added to the sign. Indeed, the seafood was fresh and the atmosphere exciting. The combination worked well and the company has since opened a second seafood restaurant and a Mexican restaurant, each of which is located in a restored historical building and has been promoted with high-art graphic billboards prior to opening.

If you rely on word-of-mouth advertising (everyone's favorite), you have to wait for people not only to try your product or service, but also to like it and tell their friends. This limits you too much when you are just starting. As your business grows, you will find that word-of-mouth is your best form of advertising, however. It costs little or nothing, and almost everyone who hears good things about your business from a friend will try it once. Advertising and public relations are more random. You are sending a message to a lot of "non-buyers." But unless yours is the only business of its kind in your community, you are setting yourself up for a lot of lean years if you just wait until the word spreads.

Consider this: Carriage Horse Livery did not advertise at first because they didn't have to. Their horse-drawn carriages on the city's streets generated enough word-of-mouth business. Competition prompted owner Wayne Scott to buy advertising, since he no longer had the only listing in the phone book.

If you own a small, labor-intensive business, like Charlie's Wood Revival furniture company, and have three months worth of back orders, you may not want to advertise. Not unless you want to expand your business, hire and train more employees and, perhaps, buy (or lease) more equipment for them to use. There aren't many businesses that don't need more business. Even though Charlie doesn't use print advertising (he tried it and it failed), he does try to build his word-of-mouth reputation by participating in a number of consumer shows in his area. He has found that executives who can touch and feel his $6,000 desks are his best customers and that they can be found at the home and office product shows.

How can you contact your future customers? With marketing.

3

MARKETING

Marketing is everything you do to sell your product or service. It includes direct sales, advertising, promotion, public relations, and publicity.

The important distinction between advertising and public relations is: advertising is most useful for getting customers in the door the first time; public relations will make them come back again and build loyalty. Advertising will cost you money; public relations (PR), for the most part, is free, unless you have a public relations specialist on your payroll. As the owner of a start-up company, you and your employees can accomplish as much as a paid professional if you learn the techniques. You should do as many jobs for your new business as you can, rather than hire people. You can and should do your own PR.

PUBLIC RELATIONS

Your advertising should make people want to try your product or service. Your ads should inform people about what you are selling and entice them to use that product or service and come to your place of business when they do. Public relations, on the other hand, should tell people about you and your company. Let the public know that behind that product or service is an interesting human being. Public relations is more than sending press releases to the newspapers to announce something new. It includes you and your employees interacting with people everywhere you go. The outcome of good PR is both publicity (i.e., newspaper articles) and more customers (who have responded to either the article or the way you behaved when you met them, say, at the Chamber of Commerce social). Whenever you have the opportunity, in print or in person, tell people about yourself, how you started your business, your goals, your employees, your motivation. A rule of small business is: people will buy from their friends. So make friends.

PROMOTION

Promotion is slightly different. Public relations should happen all the time, and it occurs in many forms. Advertising should be targeted to a specific audience and sell a specific item; whereas public relations—and its offshoot, publicity — should make people feel good enough about your business that they will shop there first, just to see if you have whatever they want. In contrast, a promotion is an event. The "Grand Opening" is the most easily identifiable form of promotion. It is limited to a fixed period of time and takes the form of a "party." Grocery stores promote anniversaries with special prices, decorations, and costumed employees. Rebates, contests, and other techniques, which encourage people to buy something because they will get something free or at a reduced price, during a limited period of time, are also promotions. Car dealers, for example, offer rebates. Radio stations entice you to listen by giving away prizes to people who call in when they hear their names announced.

SELLING

Selling encompasses all of the above. Every time you or an employee comes in contact with a customer, he or she is advertising, promoting, and doing public relations for your business. As you may have guessed, these things can work for or against your success. Just as they all have the power to attract attention and customers, they also have the ability to repel. People are harder to control than ads or promotional events. Successful public relations techniques, like sales techniques, can be learned. Buy a book on public relations or take a class. Then teach your employees how to treat customers. The outcome of public relations resembles good salesmanship without "the close." If you use appropriate PR techniques, your salespeople will have an easier time "closing the sale" because they will deal with people who are already receptive to their message, who have been pre-sold.

ADVERTISING

Can you do your own advertising? Yes and no. Since every ad agency I know works to design the ad that will suit the client, you are always "doing your own." But a professional has skills that you probably don't, including artistic ability, a familiarity with typography, and knowledge of what type of customer reads or watches which medium. No matter how talented your sons or daughters are in art, if you can tell an amateur drew your ad, the public can too.

Is advertising necessary? I would say yes, always. How much advertising is necessary is another matter. As I said before, you can spend years waiting to be discovered, or you can just get the word out. When you have all the business you can accommodate, and you decide you don't wish to expand any further ... and your sales are mostly (75 - 80%) from repeat customers

... then you should decide whether to eliminate or cut back on your advertising. The danger is, customers change. They move out of state; they lose jobs and stop shopping for a time; they are enticed by someone else's ad. So if you have a local business, you have to pay attention to the dynamics of the marketplace.

The best way to handle advertising is to budget for it. Allocate a fixed dollar sum, or a percentage of annual sales (based on projections in the first year, and actual dollar amounts thereafter), then spend that money on advertising throughout the year. Advertising, like rent and utilities, should be viewed as overhead.

A lot of small businesses stop advertising when times are tough, like the month of January. They justify it by saying, "Well, Christmas is when I do most of my business and January is bad, so I won't advertise." Maybe business is bad because they don't advertise. McDonald's sells billions of hamburgers because they spend millions of dollars on advertising. They are always telling you their name and that they sell hamburgers. Say the word "hamburger" to a small child and he or she will probably ask to go to McDonald's. Remember, Christmas is an unusual time of the year. It breaks all the rules about how and why people shop!

People buy something when they have a need for it.

Not to say that everything we buy is useful or necessary. We need some things for survival: food, clothing, and shelter. Other things we need for rewards, like collectibles, furniture, and entertainment. And then there are gifts we need for special occasions. Christmas is an occasion. People spend lots of money, retailers often make 25 to 50% of their annual income in these three months. Then we return to the other categories of need: necessity and reward. That's when all those Christmas checks from parents and grandparents get spent. We pay some bills; then we reward ourselves with things we wanted (and didn't get for Christmas). But don't plan your advertising around good and bad months. Advertising should *build an image* for your business.

Clair Hale, owner of Clair's Hallmark, has an advantage. Hallmark does a lot of image advertising; it sponsors some excellent television programming and the ads are as entertaining as the shows. So Clair has the advantage of having the Hallmark name next to his own.

Consider The Ringmaker or Mrs. Cavanaugh's Candies. Guy's and Marie's business names convey what they sell, but they must compete with dozens of similarly named businesses. Both have learned to advertise regularly with artwork and copy that set their businesses apart from the competition. While Guy and Marie know the difference between their products and the competition's (handmade vs. mass-produced; hand-dipped vs.

machine-made), the public would never know unless someone (or something) told them. So these two businesses are building images. Mrs. Cavanaugh started in 1972 and now has five stores and five department store outlets, which testifies to her success. Guy started in 1983; but his clientele grew and the fact that he was still in business after five years, when statistically most start-ups fail, testifies to the effectiveness of his marketing strategies.

Carriage Horse Livery offers horse and carriage rides in downtown Salt Lake City. For the first three years, the only advertising Wayne Scott, president, used was a sign on the back of each carriage that showed people whom to call. Since his business was one-of-a-kind, anyone who looked up "Horse and Carriage Rides" in the Yellow Pages was going to find Carriage Horse Livery. As soon as he had competition, he began advertising in local magazines so that the name Carriage Horse Livery stuck in people's minds.

When Wayne and his family started the business, they received a gift: an abundance of free publicity. They didn't have to do any public relations work to attract this publicity. Their business was such an attractive addition to the city that reporters sought them out. Anyone who wrote: "Go see the 250,000 Christmas lights on Temple Square," was certain to include a line like: "in a horse and carriage." (I did.) Since Carriage Horse Livery was the only horse and carriage company in town, this type of generic mention did it lots of good. By 1988, not only did Wayne have competition, he had expanded his "product line" to include a horse-drawn sleigh, hay wagons, and a tour trolley. Since hay and sleigh rides don't have high visibility on city streets, Wayne had to let people know they existed and entice people to try them. In addition to magazine advertising, the company now works to attract the publicity it used to get all the time—now Wayne wants the company's name mentioned in the story. One of his drivers also works as a marketing and public relations manager. She contacts writers and encourages them to write stories about the company. Sometimes ads and stories are negotiated as a package deal (which is how I came to write about them).

The advantage of public relations over advertising is that it attracts a different kind of attention and reaction. An effective ad will let people know your company's name, location, phone number, and product or service. An article can also tell a reader something about the business owner and his employees, his family, his or her "success." An article is more likely to be remembered because it commands more attention. People have to spend time reading it. Most ads merit only a quick glance. People tend to patronize their friends, and an article about the people behind the business fosters that type of relationship.

THE COMPETITION

In today's world of information overload and fast-forward video, advertisements have to compete harder to get noticed at all. Hallmark, McDonald's, Pepsi, and Coke commercials tell stories designed to make you laugh, cry, or gasp. But if you have a limited budget or a column inch, it's hard to use these techniques. Small businesses with little start-up capital can't afford this type of "production." You can, however, afford to spend your time on public relations, which could attract a professional writer to do almost the same thing for free. A story in a local magazine or paper about you and your business can attract just as much new business for your company as does an elaborate commercial on national television for a national company.

FREE PUBLICITY

How do you find writers who will do this for you? You don't; you just do something to attract their attention. First, you or your business must be of some genuine interest. If you are just starting out, forget it. There's nothing to write about. If you have been in business for at least two years, or are planning a public event — a promotion — then you have a chance. Writers want to know what you have accomplished in your business career, not about all your great plans for the distant future. There are several acceptable ways to let writers know about you.

Press Releases

The press release is a short (one page or less) typewritten statement about you and your business that is directed to the appropriate editor of your local newspaper or regional magazine. Direct your press releases with appropriate information that will let an editor know that your story would fit perfectly in his or her section of the paper or magazine. If you have invented a new product, or have increased your service from two horses and carriages to ten carriages all reproduced by the Amish, eighteen horses, two hay wagons, a sleigh, and, new this year, a horse-drawn trolley, you should let the business editor and the entertainment editor know. The growth of your company is business news. The trolley is fodder for an entertainment story.

Business Profile

You can also ask your local, regional, or city magazine editor, who has a business profile section, how you can be considered for a story. Chances are a salesperson will call. An ad combined with a feature story is the best advertising dollars you will ever spend.

About the interview: If you can help it, don't rehearse. As a writer, I know that everyone I interviewed has an "agenda." They will tell me certain things whether I ask or not. I am going to hear a commercial or, even less pertinent to a feature story, a temporary situation. Such news items are not important to my magazine readers because by the time we publish, the news will not be news. Furthermore, some news items tend to be very negative. I've gotten in long discussions with people about how rotten and unethical the competition is. But I would never print that information in a single-interview business feature story. If I did use the information in a story for a newspaper, I would call the competition to hear their side of the story, too.

My favorite interviews, which turn out to be my best stories, happen when people answer the questions that I ask. I want to know a business owner's background, how he or she got into this line of work, how the company survived, expanded, prospered ... and what kind of people work there and how they are treated. If the business is at least two years old, the owner will have absolute answers to these questions. If the business is just starting, the owner won't have a clue. Try not to waste a writer's time on a business profile story if you don't have anything insightful to say.

Business Opening

Still, even if you are just starting a business, that's news. Every town likes to boast about new business openings. You can probably get a paragraph in the town's business paper by letting them know you exist; a letter or phone call will do. Don't expect more than an announcement: "So-and-so is open for business in such-and-such a place." On the other hand, if you have just opened a one-of-a-kind business that is of entertainment value to the community, expect a lot of attention. Waterslide parks; theater and dance troupes; or an entertainment mall housing a bowling alley, roller rink, baseball batting cages, and video games will attract a lot of attention from entertainment editors and writers. Don't limit your contacts to the major newspapers in your area. They will probably give you a story at some point in time, but for constant coverage look to the giveaway papers. Every large city has an alternative newspaper or a weekly subscription paper; their writers are hungry for arts and entertainment stories. Many free or local papers are freelance written, and the key is to find the individual who is in charge of the type of entertainment you offer — like the theater editor or the "miscellaneous" editor. Put that person on your mailing list and send short letters (or press releases) about events your business sponsors. Many freelance writers write for lots of papers and magazines. So if you get to this source, the word is likely to spread.

Don't be boring. If you own a waterslide park, don't send a letter once a week telling a writer you are open for business from 9:00 a.m. to 9:00 p.m.

and you charge $5.00 admission. Once is enough. Then send another letter when your season ends or if you're having a special promotion (i.e., two for one admission on a holiday). If you're representing a theater company or an art gallery, a letter about every show is appropriate. Don't send articles; write just a paragraph or two with the name, title, address, and phone number of a contact person in the upper righthand corner. If an editor wants an article from you, he or she will probably ask for it or assign a staff writer. If you have a public relations person on staff who is trained to do this type of writing, then sending full-length articles to newspapers can work. Just make certain that every story you send is different from every other story. If one paper sees a competitor print the exact same story, you will never get coverage again from that editor. You can use the same facts, just write it with a different slant.

Don't expect to see your (or your writer's) name on the story either. When you send a press release to a newspaper or magazine, it becomes the equivalent of "notes."

For small newspapers, like Salt Lake's *The Event*, you can add a paragraph of description to your time, date, and place press release. Freelance writers usually get paid by the inch (or word), and they are quick to pad their columns or stories if the information is close at hand.

TAP AVAILABLE RESOURCES

To discover publicity resources in your town, learn to collect. Visit your convention and visitors' bureau and Chamber of Commerce. Check the information counter at your city mall. Watch the newsstands for giveaway papers. Pick up everything. Do this around the first of each month and you'll find out who will print stories about what you sell or do.

State travel councils print a lot of material that is distributed to tourists. Make your hotel, motel, river rafting company, restaurant, helicopter service, etc., known to this organization too. You will probably end up in print for several reasons. First, travel councils exist to promote tourist facilities and attractions in the state. Second, regional magazines use information supplied by the travel council to compile calendar information and write stories of interest to locals as well as tourists. Non-profit and ethnic organizations that hold annual fairs and festivals should always contact the travel council, a year in advance if possible, then send an update about four months before the event takes place.

For-profit companies are at a disadvantage here. Magazines readily give publicity to fairs and festivals, theater and art, since they are things that the general public is invited to "do." The day-to-day operation of a business is not a participation sport. Still, you can create an event. Art gallery owners have opening receptions for their artists. These two-hour wine and cheese affairs cost thousands of dollars. They require staffing, invitations and mailing costs, food, wine, etc. But they get listed in local papers. Inscapes Institute celebrated its first year of business with an art competition and a Windham Hill concert that attracted a lot of free publicity from local publications for a relatively obscure organization.

Remember, the public is easily bored. You can't just open your doors and expect people to drop by your gift shop to watch your employees at work. You have to give them some reason to come, and a corporation's president announcing anything is not a reason. Corporate presidents should do less "announcing" and more business that would attract the media's attention.

WHAT IS *NOT* AN EVENT

Just remember, a sale is not a promotional event worthy of newspaper coverage. It is common and boring copy. If you intend to promote a sale, buy advertising space. But if you are trying to promote your company's image—its contribution to the good of the community—then think of a way to attract attention. Generally speaking, people like to eat. Serving food at any affair is well advised. Salt Lake's local art galleries used to team up with catering businesses for their annual "Gallery Stroll." The attendance was better. And while some people will come for the food (not the art), you never know at what time in the future someone will have a need for original artwork in a home or office. Exposure can foster interest (or "perceived need").

The Salt Lake Area Chamber of Commerce has a monthly open house for its members. Different member organizations sponsor each month's event. Restaurants and hotels typically provide both a meeting place and food. Office buildings and community facilities team up with catering services to sponsor these get-togethers. During two hours of handshaking and business card exchanging, the food is usually the main topic of conversation. Does it generate new business for the hosts and the attendees? Definitely; although the return on one's investment of time and money may be years away.

THE CONSUMER'S REACTION TO ADVERTISING

As a business owner, you have to get away from what I call the "coupon mentality" when you are doing publicity and advertising. A misconception among entrepreneurs is that in order to justify the cost of advertising, it has to produce sales *right away*. The idea that a person decides to buy something just because he or she saw an ad is ludicrous. Why not ask yourself how you react to advertising? Be honest. Also, take a look at your own shopping behavior pattern.

Some people shop all the time for the joy of it. The ones I know are: wealthy, usually female, not spending money they earned, have lots of free time and no full-time job, and consider shopping a sport, much like golf or tennis. They also attend a lot of social functions so their new purchases can be used immediately or nearly so. So, if you are selling high fashion women's dresses, an ad featuring the latest designer original in stock should generate some business. Even so, many women who used to spend their days in shopping malls now have jobs or careers. They simply don't have as much time to shop as they (or their mothers) did.

The rest of the people I know consider shopping a chore, much like dusting and vacuuming. They shop out of *need*. There is "real need" and "perceived need." "Real need" motivates purchases of food, makes us pay our rent/mortgage and utility bills on time, and prompts us to go to the clothing store when the things we are wearing become baggy, saggy, or threadbare. "Perceived need" is illustrated best by the way teenagers shop. They tell their parents they "have to have stone-washed jeans" or they "will be rejected" by their peers. There is no survival motive here. Teenagers are affected by a great deal of social motivation. Another example of perceived need is when people make purchases to reward themselves, say, for working hard, accomplishing a goal, or just to make themselves "feel better."

I am a collector and will often ignore my real needs (for new clothing) in favor of my perceived needs (to add to my collections). The habit dates back to childhood when I "rewarded" myself with porcelain figures whenever the family went on vacation. I have quite a collection of $1.50 animals. They represent fond memories. The reward was for saving my allowance. I still play the same game. When I owned my own business, Midnight Oil Typesetting, and my profit for the month exceeded the average, I would purchase something for my collection. My purchases these days cost more since I now reward myself with limited editions and original artwork. By surrounding myself with these things, I have tangible evidence of my hard work, of my success. And when Budd and I travel or celebrate an anniversary, he'll often buy me a piece for my collection — a reminder of a good time, a reward for our relationship's success.

Except for groceries, basic clothing, and shelter, people who make a moderate living aren't quick to make major purchases. Things like furniture, appliances, electronics, and automobiles require huge outlays of cash. Let's face it, Americans don't save much. We are not a frugal people; we buy things on credit. But responsible people still want to know that they can afford the monthly payments. Others will just "save up."

The Decision-Making Process

Another reason people don't run out and react to your advertisement right away is that most people who make major purchases for their residence, like appliances and furniture, aren't single decision-makers. Just the fact that someone owns a house implies couplehood, perhaps children. (Although there are more and more single people who are buying homes for the peace and quiet they can provide.) So, husband and wife, roommates, mother and daughter have to agree on: 1) spending the money, and 2) what style they want. This takes time!

Once those decisions are made and the money is saved or budgeted, people wait for "the sale." So, while it may appear that your store is crowded with spontaneous shoppers when you run your half-price sale of the century, most of your customers have probably planned to make such a purchase for months or years, and yours just happens to be the best deal they could find during that time. Consider tires. Did you buy tires on sale because you needed tires, or because they were on sale? Both. You would have paid full price if you had to replace a blown-out tire. But when the treads looked thin, you started to pay attention to tire stores and tire ads.

Sure, some people make spontaneous purchases. We buy lots of things with very little advance planning. Small items or gifts, snack food, for instance. Sometimes the right price can trigger a perceived need — move it from the subconscious to the conscious. Windfalls, like tax rebates and a jackpot in Las Vegas, can trigger spontaneous spending. The rich spend less time considering purchases than those people of moderate means. But most people respond to "perceived needs" by planning purchases; they know if they wait long enough, most things go on sale.

For less costly items, like a birthday card or a nice dinner out, the planning period may be shorter. Plans usually center around a birthday, an anniversary, or just the need to treat oneself after an especially hard week. Most people eat out in their favorite places all the time. They've heard good things about a restaurant from a friend, tried it, and now go there every time they want that type of food. We have our favorite steak place, Chinese food place, and three Mexican restaurants. The one we patronize depends on what we plan to eat: chili verde burritos, nachos, or fajitas.

People who behave out of habit are the hardest to reach with advertising, *but the most worthwhile targets*. While your special sale on couches will attract all the couch shoppers of the moment, most of those people will be looking for the best deal on dining room tables the next time they are ready to shop for furniture. The few who have decided to decorate their entire home in the style of furnishings your store carries (contemporary, traditional, antique) will come back every time they add a piece if your products are unique. Even habitual diners do get bored, eventually, and if they have seen an ad for your restaurant, they may actually try it one day. If they like it, they are yours forever. Budd and I tried a new steak place once. We'd walked by their place of business on the way to the movie theater for what we thought was a year and remembered "reading" something about it. When we asked our waiter how long the restaurant had been in business, he said five years!

Examine your own shopping habits. When you plan to make a major purchase, or go out for a fancy dinner, don't you ask your friends about their experiences? Aren't you more likely to patronize a place with a good reputation? Of course you are.

Reinforcing Your Name and Message

Advertising helps reinforce the message. The more people hear and see the name of your business — the more familiar your business seems — the more likely they are to go there in response to a real or perceived need. Word-of-mouth is the best advertising a restaurant or retail store can have. But it's not enough.

The purpose of advertising is to reach those people who have needs. If you are selling the basic necessities, you have to reach "real need." Grocery stores advertise their "low prices" and "neighborhood convenience." These ads are directed at some basic motivations.

If you are starting a small business, however, you are more likely to be selling something that people don't "really need," but rather something that you would like them to "want," which means that you have to create or cater to "perceived need." When perceived need reaches the ready-to-buy stage, you want people to equate your business with the product that will satisfy the need. Like hamburger "means" McDonalds, Guy Lester wants jewelry to mean The Ringmaker, and Marie and George want chocolates to mean Mrs. Cavanaugh's. Clair and Twila Hale have made their Hallmark stores mean cards and gifts. The latter is their own doing; Hallmark does not make all of their giftware.

This means that you must remind people that your business exists, what you have in stock to sell, and what good service, fair prices, and high quality customers will get when they buy from you. Your advertising and promotions should convey the message that anyone who buys what you have to sell will be better off for having done so.

Of course, you can't promise or guarantee that someone will be happier, be more admired, or have more fun, but you *can* create the feeling that buying things is part of happiness and success. Just look at those popular girls and boys in the television commercials for colas and cars. It is an American fact of life that people who strive for success measure success, to some degree, in terms of material wealth and possessions.

Is this good? Bad? I believe that it is both. But it is business. And as an entrepreneur, that is what you are participating in — the buying and selling of goods and services. From this comes all the other things — jobs, abundance, even charity. It's the wealthy who have created funds and foundations to assist the arts and the poor, not us middle or lower income folk. We, psychologically, are still "getting by." The wealthy can afford to reach out into the community and do some social good. As a business person, you should aspire to be one of them. You should want to be wealthy! If getting by is good enough, you are in danger of making serious errors in how you run your business. The most important "error" you will make is how you treat and reward your employees.

If getting by is good enough for you as the owner of the company, then you won't have much cash left to pay or reward your hard-working, productive employees. If you are "getting by," they will be poor. Which means they will quit, and you are going to spend a great deal of time training new people who are willing to be poor for a while just to get the opportunity to be trained. Once you do that, they'll be working for your wealthy competitor who has enough cash flow and business sense to reward and keep good employees.

WHAT YOUR EMPLOYEES CAN DO

Employees can do more for your business than collect money from customers and put it in the register. Whatever else you do to attract customers, whether you advertise or get free publicity, whether you spend a lot of money on promotion or very little ... the way your employees treat your customers is *everything*. Good employees will make you rich. Bad ones will put you out of business. And good employees expect (and deserve) to be paid well. Why do they deserve it? Simple. The good ones are the reason you have been able to get rich. As I said in Chapter 1, if you are selling your own time, the amount of profit you will make is limited by the hours in the day. If you sell other people's time, profits can increase. This not only applies to the products you sell, but to the amount of help you can afford to hire to help you sell and/ or produce those products. It goes beyond the simple equation of more people can produce and sell more. Good employees sell and produce more than poor employees. Why? They work harder, or "smarter," to get more done in the same amount of time. And they treat customers so well that those customers come back to do business with them.

How do you recognize the "good employees"? Don't assume that someone who is always "busy" is working hard. In fact, these people may have learned to put on a show whenever you are watching. Or they may not understand how to use the equipment to its capacity. They get the job done, but slowly. Take word processing, for example. A typist can center a headline with an electronic typewriter by counting characters and backspacing halfway from center before typing, or by pressing the "code" and "center" keys and allowing the machine to center automatically. Both methods get the job done. But which employee is giving you your money's worth in productivity?

The people who "run out of things to do" should catch your attention. The measure of good work is productivity, not busyness. Watch how your employees behave. As long as a single customer is on the sales floor, your staff does have something to do. Who tries to help the customer? Other tasks also need to be done for a business to run smoothly. Shipments have to be unpacked and put away, paperwork needs attention. There is also a difference between those who "run out of things to do" and those who avoid unpleasant tasks, like paperwork or dusting. You simply have to pay attention to your employees' work habits and their priorities. Dusting does not take precedence over customer service. If you measure (and pay) your sales manager on commission, but require that person not only to sell but to solve problems and to keep your shelves dusted and displays in order, you can't measure productivity by sales figures alone. You have to examine the sum total of work accomplished. Some jobs are task-oriented, like publishing a magazine. Productivity is, in part, measured by your staff's success in meeting deadlines. At the end of each day, examine what your employees have accomplished. Some things may not be obvious or measurable, like problem solving. You have to be observant to determine which employees are able to solve problems as they arise, on their own, without taking up your time.

Good employees learn to work "smart," not constantly. They'll find more efficient ways to get the same thing done. When I was a yeoman in the U.S. Coast Guard, stationed in New Orleans, I had a finite number of letters to type and forms to process. When I got my work done for my boss, I pitched in for the other yeoman in the department, and occasionally did work for the admiral (since I was one of three people in the building who could read his handwriting). I still ran out of things to do. When my commander was promoted to captain, he continued his lunchtime ritual of returning to our office to do crossword puzzles with his former staff. I started to notice that my new commander and his captain would allow me not only to take an hour for lunch, they allowed me an additional hour to participate in the office puzzle session. Of course, if some task arose that needed immediate attention, I'd stop playing and get back to work. The commanding officer (captain) let me have my free time, and I got several promotions. (In the military a promotion is also a pay raise.)

Fred Blackburn rewarded my productivity with an offer to form a partnership, with me as managing partner. In contrast, my employer at the publishing company, Edna, berated me when I ran out of things to do. My job was to produce the editorial content of the company's magazines and catalogs by press deadline. I was given one week of formal training on a computerized typesetting program and taught the same system to an assistant three months later. After six months, I had learned all the shortcuts — all the editing tools and backup systems that the computer's software was designed to give me. My assistant, Charlene, did a lot of backspacing and retyping. So I had more free time.

Edna, sadly, did not know the difference. As time progressed, her company increased its capacity from a single monthly magazine to five periodicals, using the same three-person production staff. The owner was able to take on more projects because her employees had learned to work faster. Unable to give raises after the second year, she gave a lecture instead. She justified not increasing pay by telling her staff that they should simply settle for the increased amount of free time they had. However, she did not, in fact, let us have our free time. She would assign pieces of her job to us to do whenever we did not "look busy." (Writers and artists often work in their heads.)

At that time, the three of us began to look for new jobs. Molly found an employer who let her control her time. Big Brothers/Big Sisters of Utah considered the time Molly spent in meetings after hours as part of her job. She was their public relations director for several years. They paid her to accomplish a task, not to punch a clock. Our assistant, Charlene, moved to California. Unable to find a new job in my field right away, I renegotiated the rules. I gained two mornings off a week during which time I could freelance-write for other local publications in order to supplement my salary, which was less than a beginning school teacher earns in Utah. And Utah has a reputation for paying teachers very little in relation to surrounding states.

You probably have people working for you who are task-oriented. Personality has nothing to do with it. The people who make you laugh, who go out to lunch with you, may or may not be your best workers. Look at the quality of the work they produce, the speed at which they do it; and if they deal with your customers, watch how that goes. Do your customers continue to do business with your store, or is it really your employees whom they come back to buy from?

Be honest; look at what really happens. Don't rely on rumor or gossip. Talk to your customers. Pay attention to results. And talk to the people who work for you. Ask them what they do and how they go about getting it done. It will let you know whom to reward and whom to keep on the payroll.

4

EMPLOYEES

It *is* possible to operate a business without employees. I did. I did not want to spend a minute of my life filling out forms for the government, like my partner Fred did for his business. But I also limited my earning capacity, and I knew it. If you know this, too, and decide to go it alone, fine. But there came a point in time when my earnings were not keeping up with my expectations, nor with the cost of living. I had to either hire someone to help me, or sell the business, or work a lot more hours. Hiring another person would have required that I buy new machinery, which meant obtaining a bank loan, going into debt, and committing to operate my business for a long time.

My partner and I had gone our separate ways by this time. So I gave some serious thought to the idea of not being in business for myself at all. I had not really chosen to be a "typesetter." The opportunity to go into business just came up. Mine was one of those Wood Revival choices — serendipity self-employment. Fred had trained me on a machine that was similar to the machine I had learned to use while in the Coast Guard. I had taken classes in layout, pasteup, and printing. While I went into a familiar line of work, starting a new business was not really my idea. It was Fred's. Since I had the skills, the figures, and a belief that self-employment was a good idea, I took the risk.

Five years later I decided I did not want to do it for the rest of my life, nor did I want to get into debt or hire employees. I wanted to stop.

Had I found a full-time job during that year, I would have closed the doors. The universe had other plans, and a former customer, Bev Miller, asked me if I had ever considered a partnership. I told her that what I really wanted to do was sell out. She bought my business.

FAMILY-RUN BUSINESSES

Bev Miller hired her daughter who had just graduated from high school. Four years later, she employed most of her family. When she purchased Midnight Oil Typesetting, her daughter was under twenty-one. Her paperwork was

---

41

minimal since minors employed by their parents don't have to pay Social Security tax. A lot of business people I know employ(ed) their children. It's an excellent way to get started.

For some reason, the government treats family-run businesses better than others. The taxes and forms are fewer, the hassles less frequent. The biggest advantage a start-up company has, if the employees are members of the same family, is the dedication. The dedication of your employees will be much greater if they feel they have a proprietary interest in what you're doing. Children who work for their parents can safely assume that Mom and Dad want them to take over the family business someday. It's a matter of time (when the parents retire) and ability (whether the kids have any). Families who work together have other advantages. Children who live at home can afford to work for less, and their parents will work harder to teach them all aspects of the business, since they have a vested interest in being patient.

Don't be surprised when the children leave your business shortly after graduating from college. They'll probably be back — at least one of them — and that's all you really need.

DO YOU NEED EMPLOYEES?

The rest of us have to deal with strangers — people who bring us résumés or whom we have met somewhere before. We have to train them without any long-term commitment on anyone's part. And we must fill out more forms. Just try to skip this task one month and find out how long you stay in business. Some people get so involved in paperwork, they run out of selling time. Make certain that hiring people will generate enough money to compensate you for the time you will spend away from the counter (or phone) selling and in the back office filling out paperwork, to justify doing it. If not, don't.

Unlike the Japanese, American employers don't expect employees to stay, and employees typically don't stay in a small business. The few who do have found a benevolent employer, a salary that they feel compensates them fairly, coworkers they enjoy, the right benefits and, for some, the ability to take and afford long vacations. Some people stay because they lack the courage or skill to seek a better opportunity elsewhere. But let's focus on your top performers.

KEEPING GOOD EMPLOYEES

Corporations tend to keep employees longer than small companies; they simply are able to pay (a lot) more money and give better benefits. People who work for large companies like it that way. They consider security important, and they don't enjoy radical change. People who work for small businesses, especially new small businesses, are motivated by different things. They are risk takers. They are usually more social and tend to make friends with the people they work with. Corporate people compete for promotions. Small business employees know that the job above theirs is the owner of the company's and, if they want that job, they'll have to go out on their own. A lot of them are there for that reason. They want to learn all they can, and if they come to believe you aren't treating them fairly, or paying them well enough, they might just become your competition.

Does this mean you should hold back information — keep them in the dark? Not at all. Because between then and now, the more they learn, the more you teach, the more they feel they are "part of the team, like family" and that their hard work will bring future financial rewards, the more money they will generate for your business and you.

Spreading the Wealth

Your most productive employees will expect to share in their own profitability. Nothing is more discouraging than when one good salesperson "makes up" for three mediocre ones, and knows it. If your company is doing well, but your star employee isn't getting his or her fair share, and knows it, you are courting disaster. That person's morale will sink, his productivity will decline, and he will start to look for opportunity elsewhere.

How much salary is enough? As I said about employers in Chapter 1, it depends on age and circumstances. It also depends on what the employee thinks he or she is "worth." Corporate employees tend to be worth more than small business employees because national/international corporations make more money. (I'm talking about successful corporations, of course.)

What an employee is really worth is a percentage of the total profit that he or she generates for your business. At the minimum, anyone on your payroll should "sell" enough to pay his or her own salary. The good ones will pay their own salary and contribute to yours. The good ones expect to be rewarded for high performance. If you are carrying a lot of poor performers on your payroll, you won't be able to hand out these rewards, because the profits your stars generate make up for those other folks.

Don't tell your star salesperson that if he "wants to earn more, just sell more," unless you, as the owner, are doing things to make this possible, and the economy is in good shape (people are buying what you have to sell). At some point he will sell all that is possible to sell in an eight-hour day. Unless you introduce a popular new product or raise your prices, your employee has peaked with your current inventory or product line.

Be honest. Be honest with yourself first. Then you'll be honest with your employees. The best ones are worth keeping. Put them on a regular salary that compensates them for their value to your company. If someone performs tasks other than selling, such as management functions, and these jobs take her off the sales floor, don't penalize her for doing more by paying her the same as your people who aren't managing.

It's hard to know how much money the editor of a magazine is worth since there are no direct sales to measure. But if the content of the magazine enables the owner and sales force to sell advertising to support the publication, the editor (and art director and production assistant) are worth a percentage of the income the company generates. Lots of staff support jobs aren't directly related to sales. But if you had to do all the work your bookkeeper or secretary does, and you as the owner are the company's primary salesperson, then you have to determine worth in another way: How much less could you sell if you had to do those jobs? And what would it cost you in management time that might cause you to be less effective if you had to do those jobs? Remember, when you started, you did everything. As your business can afford it, you hire help so you can spend your time more productively. These staff people become part of the overhead, like rent and utilities. Their presence enables you and your other salespeople to be more effective, which generates income and profits. These support people are "worth" a percentage of the total profitability of your company because they enable you to do things to generate income, rather than handle so many necessary, but not revenue-producing, chores.

LIMIT YOUR PAYROLL

Don't hire support personnel too soon. Again, if you are just starting, you have to be your own secretary and bookkeeper. You have to limit your payroll to the number of people who have skills that will let you run your business. You must be your own salesperson even if it isn't one of your skills, when you start. No one else will work as hard or as long to build your business as you (and possibly your family). You should do your own bookkeeping because if you hire someone too soon, you will lose touch with your business. You will be so busy trying to get clients that you won't have time to look at the books; and since someone else will be doing them, you won't understand the necessity of doing so. You have to do the books; you must know how much money your business is generating every day. You must be in touch with receivables, payables, and cash flow. If you don't have (make) the time, or don't like the chore, you'll go broke because you'll make decisions based on the assumption that everything is fine all the time. This is never true. And it's especially never true for a company just starting out.

HIRE ONLY THE PEOPLE YOU NEED

When you start, hire only those people whose skills will enable you to keep your business in operation. Do as much of the work as you know how; and do all of the managerial functions — record keeping, bill paying, capital expenditure decision-making. As the business prospers, you must reward those people who helped you launch your company. Don't hire more people because you don't want to do your own bookkeeping. You need to put that money into the paychecks of the people who got you where you are, because when they started with you they took a big risk, and they probably accepted a salary that was a lot less than they are "worth." The risk they took was that you might fail. They need monetary evidence that you are not failing. They need regular raises as your profitability increases. They have become highly skilled since you hired them. They are part of the reason that you have stayed in business this long. That means they are of value, and money will keep them in your employ a little longer.

Bonuses are nice, but don't get salary and bonuses confused. One is regular and can be counted on, the other is a once in a while treat. If you give symphony tickets to someone as a bonus, it is possible that someone other than your employee benefited from them.

RAISES

How do you determine raises? Again, it depends on how profitable your company is. The people who participate in a company's growth should share in that growth in proportion to their contribution. If you don't pay them what they are worth, or can't, they will leave. That's okay, too. But you will have to start over and hire someone new. New people take three to six months to learn your inventory or the work system — the equipment, how to deal with the other employees, where everything is kept. They will not pay their way soon. Don't expect it. But people who are your highest performers are worth keeping. If you can't afford to give them raises then look at your business and ask yourself why not. The answer may give you an insight into some chronic problem that endangers the survival of your company. Are you doing business on trade? Have you sold an enormous amount on credit and failed to collect? Have you expanded so fast, or hired so many people, that you are short of cash — are unprofitable?

What are you doing? Stop doing it! Cut back. Mend your ways and get back to business. The purpose of business, remember, is to make money.

DON'T DELEGATE MANAGEMENT CHORES

As your business grows and your bottom line tells you that you have money available to hire help, be careful which chores you delegate. If you are your company's best salesperson and dislike management — hiring, firing, bidding, collections, keeping track of and managing cash flow and credit — you will be tempted to hire someone to do those chores. You see them as chores, and as such you won't assign the responsibility that goes along with the chores, just the chores. The "chore" is writing figures in a ledger, or typing numbers from sales contracts into a computer then printing out aging charts. The "responsibility" is the power and authority to decide when and how to use the money that flows through your company. You'll still want to do that part, but you'll begin to do it part-time, which is not often enough.

If you hire someone to do the chore, make certain that he or she also has advisory skills and authority. Make certain that you listen to what he tells you about your financial condition. Use that information and keep yourself well enough informed so that every moment of every day you know how much you owe and who owes how much to you. Know your costs and prices. Again, every moment of every day. Your prices have to include your real costs of doing business. Suppliers change their prices; you have to react quickly to remain profitable.

Sure you can delegate, but if you don't have the information you need to base decisions on at your fingertips, then you have failed to "manage." You will be tempted to place blame. "So-and-so didn't get me all the figures I asked for." Never mind. If your bookkeeper isn't doing the job you need done, find another bookkeeper. But make certain that you keep the books current in the meanwhile, or you will make decisions based on old, erroneous information. You will set prices based on old costs, and you may go broke.

The point is: never delegate management functions. You can hire help, but the responsibility ultimately belongs to the boss. You may enjoy selling more, but to stay in business, to become a profitable business, you have to manage. If you don't want to, go to work for someone who does.

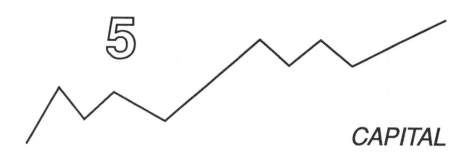

CAPITAL

The "experts" will tell you that the reason the United States is in a major recession is debt. We import more than we export; we spend more than we earn. The same principle applies to your personal finances and your business. When you overextend yourself by committing to make payments on more goods and services than you can afford, you're likely to go broke. Still, credit has enabled the developed nations to enjoy a wealth of goods and services. Credit allows a small business to grow into a big business, if it is not abused.

DETERMINING YOUR START-UP CAPITAL

When you start your business, you may not be allowed to play the credit game as would businesses that have histories. They can purchase supplies, then pay the supplier in fifteen to thirty days. This enables the owner to collect money from customers — cash from direct sales and "receivables" from credit customers — and use that income to pay the bills ("payables") rather than using "start-up capital" (the money invested in the business to get it started). As a new business, you'll need "working capital" (which may include income and start-up capital). You'll be expected to pay cash for inventory, for supplies, and for some equipment, unless you lease your equipment. You might be able to purchase some of these things and make time payments, but you'll have to make those payments whether your business is making sales or not. So you need working capital — the cash money it takes to keep your business in operation — to pay for day-to-day expenses.

Most businesses fail because they don't have enough money when they start. Building a business takes years. The early years will cost you more than later years. You'll spend money on desks and filing cabinets, computer systems, and training employees, to name a few. You'll need to advertise more in the early years to get the word-of-mouth advertising started. Chances are, in the first year or two, everyone will be paid except you, the owner. So part of your capital needs will be what you require to live on. The SBA prints a number of useful pamphlets on starting a business. Read them.

THE FORMULA

When you start, you are going to have to take an educated guess about how much money you will need. Here's my basic formula:

- Money I need to *live on*:
- Payroll:
- Social Security and Unemployment Tax:
- Supplies for production/Inventory costs:
- Office supplies:
- Fees, dues, professional publications or memberships that relate to doing business or promoting the business:
- Insurance for the company (liability):
- Insurance for the employees and myself (health, dental, life):
- Annual tax-preparation fee for CPA:
- Production equipment:
- Office furniture:
- Rent and utilities:
- Phone:
- Advertising:

Here's how to determine the numbers:

As I said in Chapter 1, many people start businesses based on their professional (or hobbyist) experience. This is the first place you need to look for numbers. If you have worked as a manager, you have certainly had access to figures. You know what things cost. Write this information down. If you are a hobbyist, your numbers will be high because you have not bought in quantity. Call the people you have bought supplies from and ask what prices they would charge for bulk purchases, say a hundred or more. If you have no background in what you plan to sell, you'll have to make a lot of telephone calls to potential suppliers.

While you're asking about prices, also ask about terms. Will you have to pay cash or make payments over time? But to determine how much capital you will need, assume you'll pay cash on delivery. It's best to calculate your money needs on a worst-case scenario — what if no one buys what you have to sell? What will it cost to open your doors for business?

Money I Need to Live On

If you have savings, or a working spouse who can support you both, put zero here. Take nothing out of your business until it can afford to pay you, and you'll have an advantage over people who are trying to make a living right away by going into business for themselves. You'll give your business a little breathing room. Investing in a business doesn't always have to be in money or personal assets (like your home computer or desk). You can invest your time. If you have to earn a living right away, figure out how much you need just to get by. If you are turning an avocation (part-time income-producing hobby or profession) into a full-time business, you will know how much you can expect to earn based on the business's track record. Still, if you plan to rent a storefront, you will also have new expenses. The principle of paying yourself what the business can afford to pay still applies.

Payroll

When you start, you should use primarily your own time to produce and/or sell your products. Hire only those people who have skills you don't have that will enable you to start a business. Pay market rates — the least you can for qualified people.

Social Security and Unemployment Tax

Employers like to ignore this to their detriment. These figures will be a percentage of your payroll. If you miss a payment, the government can close you down. Don't get taxes confused with working capital; keep it in the bank, along with the sales taxes you collect, so you can pay it when due.

Supplies for Production/Inventory Costs

Find out what supplies you will have to buy, right away, to produce a product if you are in a service or manufacturing business. For retail, determine how much inventory you need in your store to attract customers. This is a good time to see what the competition is doing, or use your professional knowledge, to estimate how much is enough. Talk to suppliers. If they think you are a potential customer, you'll be surprised how much information they have about how much of what you will need to get started. They want your business and they want you to succeed. If you do, they'll have a new, steady customer.

Office Supplies

The needs are basic. To start, you'll probably need a few desks and file cabinets, paper, pens, staplers, and such. Do you need a photocopy machine? Wait until your monthly bill at the photocopy store is so high that it would be cheaper to own your own. Also, don't generate paperwork for the file cabinets. Be frugal when you start. If you can tell someone to do something in person, and watch her write it down, don't be so quick to copy an office memo that contains the same information. Don't let paper replace your weekly staff meeting. It's easier but costs more and produces less.

Fees, Dues, Professional Publications or Memberships

Lots of salespeople are going to flock to your door to sell you trade magazines and professional memberships. Which ones do you really need? The ones that you are going to read. Don't buy stuff for the table; only for your education. Memberships in professional organizations are only worthwhile if you can promote your business as a result. If it's just for the résumé, forget it. If it will attract customers or generate business, consider it part of your advertising and promotion budget. For example, the Salt Lake Area Chamber of Commerce offers a monthly after-hours social, which enables business people to meet, greet, and exchange business cards. If your business is the type of business that could benefit from this activity, and you have the time to go to all these social functions, then join. Don't do it just for the free food or for a plaque on your wall. Ask people who are members of various associations about their experiences.

Insurance

Call an insurance agent and find out what you'll need to insure your office equipment and furniture, and insure you against liability (should someone, for example, slip on the sidewalk in front of your store). Also, find out about health and dental insurance rates. If you are starting out with fewer than ten employees, this is going to be outrageously expensive and hard to get. Can you do without? If you and your employees are covered by a spouse's plan, yes. But if you and your employees are single, or not covered, it's going to cause problems. It's one of those minimum benefits that good people shop for when they are looking for employment. You might be able to join an association and qualify for group rates. Ask your agent.

Tax Preparation Fee

Certified Public Accountants (CPAs) provide professional advice for the new business that is operating ethically. Lawyers solve problems. If you want to avoid a lot of problems, hire a CPA right away. Have him or her set up your accounting system, which can be as simple as categories on a green ledger sheet. For a fixed fee, your CPA should agree to provide tax forms and reports, as required, for the IRS and the state; and notify you when and how much tax you owe for quarterly payments, Social Security, and unemployment insurance payments. You should do the rest of your information collection and analysis yourself at first. As your company grows, you might consider using other professional accounting services, like bookkeeping on a time-share computer system to generate reports and analyses.

Don't try to do without a CPA unless you are one or have a strong background in accounting (or the law). It's easy to forget tax time when you are running a new company. If you get better at figuring out these forms and are good at remembering when to pay, then do it yourself and fire your accountant.

Production Equipment

I've separated this from office equipment to distinguish the essential from the optional. "Production equipment" refers to machinery or tools you'll need in order to run your business or produce your product. A baker needs an oven and a refrigerator; a typesetter needs a typesetting machine; a retail store needs a cash register. This doesn't imply newness or state-of-the-art, necessarily — just what you need to stay competitive in the industry. A publishing company does not have to have a typesetting machine or a printing press. This work can be subcontracted. But you should analyze the cost of doing so versus the cost of having your own equipment. Select whichever is less or will produce a higher return.

You'll have to reevaluate your needs over time. You might want to add production equipment to your business gradually. In my typesetting business, I subcontracted PMTs (stats) until I had a high enough demand to justify purchasing my own equipment (and film). I also bought a used camera, which I had to hand-crank to set the enlargements and reductions. Push-button, motorized machines were available, but I couldn't see any revenue-producing benefit.

If you do too much too soon, you'll end up in too much debt. How will you know? You can't always; you have to make an educated guess.

Office Furniture

These things have nothing to do with making or selling a product or service. An old door across two saw horses will serve as a desk. My first office chair was a straight-backed wooden thing, and I sat on a phone book for three years. I used profits to buy a cushiony swivel chair. My furniture was hand-built by a friend of my partner. Most of my file cabinets and supply shelves were garage-sale finds. As I earned profits, I replaced only what needed replacing. I didn't think sitting on the phone book was reasonable, but garage-sale cabinets still held my paper and pencils just fine. I used profits to buy new fonts and eventually to buy a headliner machine and the aforementioned stat camera—all of which could generate more income, not just hold supplies.

Consider this: What if you fail? How much stuff do you need to make your business work? What other stuff is for your creature comfort or just for show? And is anyone looking? Your front office may command matching furniture, so customers don't get the impression yours is a fly-by-night operation. But the back shop could do with less. Spend most of your start-up capital on things that will generate income; very little on things for show. You don't need artwork on the walls, or $50 ferns hanging from the ceiling. Bring things from home to decorate your office. If the display is an integral part of making the sale, like Guy's The Ringmaker, fine walnut cabinets may be appropriate. But oak cabinets stained to look like walnut will have the same impact on the customer's perception of your merchandise. If you can make deliveries in your 1960 truck, don't rush right out to buy the latest model delivery van. Use your excess profits for that at some future time. On the other hand, don't be so cheap that your employees get discouraged. A broken chair can cause back problems; poor lighting, eye strain. Be realistic.

Rent and Utilities

Determine how much space you'll need and what location will give your business a chance to succeed. The cute storefront on a side street near the major shopping center downtown may offer cheap rent. But the mall sells high foot traffic. Ask yourself: Is what I'm selling so unusual or so needed that people will seek me out no matter where I locate; or am I offering a product or service similar to (though better than) the others so that high exposure will be of greater value? Walk through the shopping malls and look at what is there: clothing, shoes, jewelry, and lots of food. Why are they all there? Because that's how the public has learned to shop for those items. They want to look at what every store has to offer, then select their favorite, or the best buy. Consider the businesses on Main Street or in neighborhood strip malls and storefronts. Some have been there since Main Street was built; they've employed three generations and own the building. Overhead is now zero, customers are regular, and they are dedicated to downtown's Main Street. They don't count.

Look at the others: photocopy shops, one-of-a-kind gift and specialty clothing stores, and more food places. Consider how a Main Street location, a block or two away from the city's two shopping malls housing some 200 stores, works for these businesses. Well, people in offices need to eat. So it's likely that they'll go to the closest restaurant for those thirty minute to an hour breaks. Photocopy shops service offices, too. They locate near office buildings and towers; customers are attracted by proximity. Specialty shops sell such unusual merchandise that people will seek them out wherever they are. "Unusual" can mean quality, product, or even price. That's why discount shopping warehouses have become so popular in the west. They offer members a huge variety of goods, at low prices, with lots of free parking, and they require a commute of some distance.

Which category does your business fit? What is the competition doing? Where do you need to locate to be competitive? Cheapest isn't always best. Look around, then call landlords or leasing agents and talk with them. Ask not only about rental prices, but also what your landlord will do, if anything, to attract people to the location. On Main Street, Salt Lake City, promotions are sponsored by a merchant's tax, which pays for an organization called the Central Business Improvement District (CBID). This group puts colorful banners on the lamp posts and helps sponsor parades and downtown events. The Chamber of Commerce and Downtown Retail Merchants Association are supported by members' dues. They also sponsor downtown promotions, like sidewalk sales and social functions.

In many malls you pay dues to a Tenant Association as part of your lease requirement. Mall management (a marketing director) uses this money to attract the public to the mall. Find out what activities your potential marketing director has planned for the upcoming year and find out what type of people patronize that mall. Mall managers conduct lots of surveys and compile lots of statistics. They know who shops in their mall, where they come from, what they shop for. Ask as many questions as you need to, to help you decide whether to locate in the mall. They want you, and the more you sound like you have done your homework and are, therefore, going to be running a viable business, the more a mall manager will be willing to work with you. Negotiate — don't be too quick to decide. Spontaneity should be reserved for vacations, not business decisions. You have to decide if your income projections justify the higher rent that a mall location calls for.

Phone

Call the phone company. A business phone will cost a lot more than a home phone. If you need more than one line because you have a sales force, contact some private phone equipment companies and get bids on installing a phone system. Find one that can accommodate additional lines without requiring all new equipment. Add the cost of installation and project your long-distance service needs.

Advertising

Again, you have to spend money to produce future revenue and it is hard to know how much is enough. So set a budget — either a fixed amount or a percentage of projected/actual sales as discussed in a previous chapter.

That's my list. You can add to it if you have other "necessities." If you have monthly figures, multiply them by twelve. That's the minimum you'll need to start a business. If, after the first year in business, you aren't generating enough income to pay these bills, something is seriously wrong. The first place to look is at your salary. Are you taking more money home than the business can afford to pay you? Now that you have a year's worth of actual figures, reevaluate. How close were your estimates to your actual costs of doing business? They should be very close. If not, which projections were inaccurate and what can you change to try to make the business more profitable?

ONE LAST STORY

Essence Perfumery's founder, Herb Davis, spent a great deal of time and money to determine how to make and market his product — copies of designer perfumes. His first retail outlet was a kiosk in a downtown mall. Later, the company opened a storefront location in a suburban mall. For all that time and effort, the kiosk closed about two years later. After an initial splash of advertising and publicity, the company retreated into invisibility.

No matter how careful you are, how much research you do, there is no absolute way to determine what the public will buy or how much they will pay for it. So the final question you should ask yourself is: Would you buy what you want to sell? If so, what would you pay for it; and where would you go to find it; or would you listen if a salesperson called?

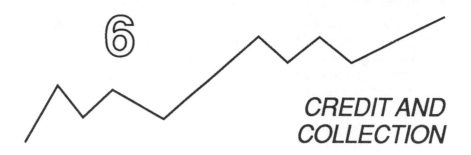

CREDIT AND COLLECTION

If you don't like to ask for money, don't go into business.

Collection starts with the sale. Retailers collect all the money when they part with their goods unless they have a layaway system, in which case they collect partial payment to hold the goods and all the money when the customer receives the goods.

Some large retail businesses, like car dealers or furniture stores, have in-house financing or credit plans. But this type of financing system is actually a business in itself. For a small start-up business it makes no sense to be in the "banking" business if your capital is limited.

Collection requires more effort for service-type businesses (and suppliers or wholesalers). As in my typesetting, Fred's printing, and Edna's publishing businesses, products were "custom made" and typically paid for upon completion and delivery.

DON'T GIVE CREDIT UNLESS
YOU KNOW YOU'LL BE PAID

The rule for retailers is: Don't let it out of the store until it is paid for. Don't listen to stories. Get identification for checks and double check signatures. In service, supply, or wholesale businesses, you can expect to deal with time payments. Why can't you just ask for cash up front? You can, but in many industries, credit has become the norm. You will be able to increase your clientele if you do extend credit. Retailers have the benefit of charge-card companies to extend credit and take the risks. Other businesses have to extend their own credit and do their own collections. Typically, the customer will receive the product before you receive payment in full. Extending credit is dangerous; be careful how you do it.

Both Fred and Edna decided they didn't want to "do collections." They said they didn't want to offend anyone, or lose customers or friends. People who don't pay their bills aren't customers, certainly not friends. They've gotten what they came for — something for nothing — and they won't be back unless you allow them to take more for the same price. Make certain you collect the money your customers owe you.

My rule, as owner of Midnight Oil Typesetting, was simple: I never gave credit to anyone unless I could personally walk to their office and sit there until I collected payment. In five years of doing business, I was the victim of two criminals (one spent time in jail; the other is under investigation by the SEC for fraud), one bounced check, and two walk-aways. A walk-away is someone who places the order and never returns to pick up the "custom made" merchandise. In a service business this is a danger because you can't, for example, take stationery apart and put the paper back on the shelf for another customer to buy.

DETECTING THE NON-PAYERS

Some people who own new businesses get so focused on getting a signature on a sales agreement that they forget to ascertain their chances of getting paid at a future date. There are ways to tell if someone doesn't intend to pay you. You can't always tell. But here are some guidelines for businesses that extend credit to their customers in the normal course of doing business.

A signature on a sales agreement is not necessarily a "sale." Some business owners who think otherwise find themselves working a lot of hours trying to collect on their receivables. Why? Because a "sale" is not a signature, but a contractual *agreement* between you and your customer to exchange goods for money at a specified point in time. If you have not explained that to your customer, you may have gotten a signature but you never got the "agreement," and you have given your client a reason (an excuse) to not want to pay you.

I saw a parade of salespeople pass through our publishing office with fists full of paperwork. But those clients never agreed to pay for an ad; they had been high pressured or sweet talked (a few thought they'd get a date with one of our salespeople) into signing a piece of paper. They started to rehearse reasons not to pay the moment the salesperson left the office. My favorite is: "I've run the ad one month and haven't gotten any calls." Does this sound familiar? Refer back to the chapter about how advertising works. Make certain you and your sales force tell your clients what they are buying. Did you promise calls? If so, you deserve not to get paid. You can't promise that. You can only promise exposure and potential increase in sales. Furthermore, not everyone calls before they visit a store. Not every caller will say: "I saw your ad in such-and-such a magazine." If you are selling something as intangible as advertising or promotion, be careful what you promise. Be even more careful about what your salespeople promise if they are paid on commission.

Deliver What the Customer Expects, When it is Expected

If you sell something more tangible, like paper to a print shop or stationery to an individual, make certain that what you deliver is what the customer *expects to receive*. This applies to any supply business. Make certain the customers are *involved* in the production process so the finished product (i.e., letterhead) looks as they expect it to. Make certain the piece goods you deliver are identical to your salesperson's sample. This is the first step in gaining "agreement."

Keep promises about time. If you plan to deliver the product in two days, don't promise one, then apologize for the delay. Customers appreciate honesty, even if you are under-optimistic. If you say three days (to give your equipment time to break down and be repaired) and the customer gets delivery in two, you're a hero. Promise two days and have the machine break down, and you're a jerk. Give yourself a realistic amount of time for production, plus a day for breakdowns and emergencies, then deliver on time.

Make certain, when you get the contract signed, that the customer understands *both what* he or she is purchasing and that you *expect to be paid*. How do you do this? SAY IT. Don't ask anyone to "read the (fine) print." They may or may not do so. They may or may not understand what they have read. Fine print is what a lawyer requires for a court battle. But if you have not gained understanding and agreement at the point of sale, your lawyer is going to have a hard time, and it will cost you a great deal to collect money that should only require a phone-call's worth of effort on your part. Simply say, "Now, you agree to pay me $___ in thirty days, that is January 5th" (use a calendar as a visual reinforcement if possible). Get a verbal agreement ("Yes.") "Then I'll receive payment on the 5th." ("Yes.") "Good. If you forget, I'll call to remind you."

Write down the dates on your own calendar and on the agreement or invoice. Then do what you said you would do. If the check does not arrive on the 5th, call and say, "You agreed to pay me today. I'll be over to collect at 3:00 p.m." You should not get any discussion if you went through the process correctly. My dates and numbers are arbitrary except for the collection time. Three p.m. is good because it gives your client time to find the paperwork, have a check typed, and get it signed by any number of people. If you wait until later in the afternoon, people start to go home.

This all should sound obvious, but it's surprising how many people overlook the obvious because of fear. Fear of not making the sale. Fear of losing a friend. Fear of talking.

REMEMBER TO WHOM YOU'RE SELLING

Which leads us to another factor about successful collections: whom you sell to.

So many people get busy getting contracts signed that they forget the process of selling. The process — it bears repeating — starts with you explaining what you're selling and its value to a potential buyer. The middle of the sale occurs when that person agrees to the item's value and expresses his or her willingness to pay for it (immediately or over time). And the end (or "close") is when you collect payment in full for merchandise delivered. Sometimes salespeople quit when they get past the first step. That's the easy part. It requires less effort and no understanding to get a signature.

So how can you tell if you are dealing with agreement, and ability and willingness to pay. Ability to pay and willingness to pay are different but related. Ability means that the debtor has the money with which to pay you. Willingness means he or she is motivated to pay you. Those who are willing may or may not be able. Those who are able may or may not be willing. You have to ascertain if your clients are both. By selling correctly — getting agreement and understanding — you will establish willingness. If you are selling on a contract and granting (in-house) credit, it is up to you as a creditor to determine your debtor's (client's) ability. Whether you have a credit application or you simply grant credit to anyone who signs your sales agreement, you can ask certain questions to help determine credit-worthiness.

LENGTH OF TIME IN BUSINESS

New businesses should pay cash. Most new businesses are undercapitalized because the owners had to spend more than they anticipated. A few planned and knew what to expect; nevertheless, a first year in business is precarious. Frequently, new retailers spend a great deal of money remodeling the interior of the store and purchasing office furniture. Statistically, a business less than a year old has a high chance of failure. The odds improve in years two through five. So, as you make the sale, you should determine ability to pay by asking your client some questions that will let you know what to expect, without causing negative feelings.

Leave your role as a salesperson and become a curious, interested, supportive fellow business person. Questions like: "How are you doing?" "How did you get started? I've always thought that would be such an interesting business," and "What did you do before this?" will help you to determine your risk. Then listen carefully. If the answer is: "I worked for a Fortune 500 company and got tired of bureaucracy, so ..." that person probably has money in the bank and some ideas about how to operate a profitable business, as well as the ability to sell and manage. Good risk. If the answer is: "I just wanted to work for myself, and going into this business sounded fun, and cheap to start ...." get cash. People who haven't given going into business much thought are not good credit risks. They will cause you grief if you let them. They are, typically, unrealistic and not prepared for hardships. They give up easily and leave creditors holding their receivables.

People who have owned profitable businesses before are a better risk than those who are trying for the first time. Even people who have failed in businesses that have operated for a number of years are better risks than those who have never tried. They should have learned a lot. If they come back for more, they plan not to make the same mistakes twice. Some people make careers of starting new businesses and selling them. These people are marginal risks. Just keep their payments current. Make certain you are paid on time by all your creditors, and don't do new work until old work is paid for in full.

LOCATION

People with storefronts or offices are better risks than those with post office boxes or those who work from home. I made it a rule never to extend credit to anyone who didn't have a place of business. It is too easy just to give up if you have not invested in a place. I assumed that these people were going to see if being in business worked; they were not necessarily going to work at being in business.

New restaurants are one of the highest risk businesses of all. The start-up costs for interior decorating and equipment are enormous compared to most retail and service businesses. In fact, any business that has had to complete its interior space, starting from the walls out, is at a high risk. The restaurant that moves into the already decorated space (after the original owner failed) is at a distinct advantage but still is a high risk. (This does not include franchises, since you have to have a lot of capital to purchase one. Franchises are an excellent credit risk.)

PAYMENT HISTORY

I never gave credit to a new client, except some I inherited from my partner Fred's print shop. After I received payments in full, on time, for a year, if someone asked me, I considered how well I knew that person and what I thought about his or her character. Obviously, people who come in once a year are hard to judge. But those customers who came in regularly — monthly or weekly — had given me ample opportunity to "chit chat" and form an impression. If I thought them to be honest and running a sound business, I extended credit. If not, I just said, "No." You have to get past the fear that refusing someone credit will lose you business. They may not do business with you, but you have not lost. Just tell yourself to let them go steal from someone else. Honest people will let you run your business however you see fit. If that means you won't extend them credit, fine. If you have something they want and value, they'll buy it from you regardless. People who try to run your business for you by telling you that everyone buys and sells on credit are not good credit risks.

KEEP DEBTS CURRENT

One more thing: The more money someone owes you, the more he or she will resent you and try to find ways to make you the enemy, so he won't have to pay at all. People don't like to owe money, especially a lot of it. So if you extend credit to someone, the most important thing you must do is to collect it when you said you would. If you let time pass or let the debt accumulate, you might lose a customer.

Lots of business owners make this mistake. Ninety days after the sale, they scramble to get paid. Meanwhile, the same client has signed more contracts and those "sales" have become due and payable, too. If you don't ask to be paid as agreed, you've put yourself in a position of trying to "collect late payments," rather than "finish the sale." While you and your client should have agreed upon how much and when to pay, you never discussed what to do if that failed to happen. So you have no agreement or willingness; you have a fight. Avoid this by following the selling process.

Non-profit, government-funded organizations and large corporations are the exception to the above. They are usually good risks and very slow to pay. They typically expect continuous service and credit from you; you can expect to be paid very slowly by them. It's surprising, but those who are most able to pay also know what they can get away with, and they do. They believe that you need their business more than they need your goods or services. If this is true, just put up with it. You will get paid, late. Count on it. Which means don't expect to have that money to spend until you receive it. A common mistake new business owners make is confusing "working capital" with "receivables." Don't make business decisions based on how much money you *should* receive in any given month based on your ledger cards ("receivables"). You can only count on having the monies that you have actually collected (working capital), or have a pattern of collecting. Never assume a large public corporation will pay you in thirty days, as your contract states, then lease a new piece of equipment which you, in turn, must pay for in thirty days. What if you don't get paid on time? You'll still owe your payment. If you are new in business, you should buy inventory and supplies, or hire new personnel, etc., based on the amount of money you have in the bank (start-up capital) and current income. After a year or two, you will have figures upon which to project your monthly income for the following year. Be conservative; buy that new piece of equipment with end-of-the year profits. If you need that piece of equipment in order to accept the contracted work from a big client, insist on getting paid in full up front. If the client balks, wait until you can pay for the equipment with cash — investment capital or profits — then seek the contract and use your own money to buy the machinery. If the contract fails or payments are slow, look for new clients. It's always better to spend your time looking for new clients and servicing existing ones than to chase old debts. The first two earn you money; the last costs you both money and mental energy.

DON'T WORK FOR THOSE WHO DON'T PAY

The final mistake creditors make is continuing to do work for people who haven't paid. Why on earth would you continue to, say, run an advertisement in your magazine for a customer who hasn't paid for the past two ads (two months)? There are, in fact, lots of explanations: optimism, trust in human nature, desperation, stupidity ... If you think that allowing people to owe you a lot of money will increase your chances of getting paid, it just isn't so. If you believe that your demonstration of good faith and trust will revive theirs, you are, indeed, an optimist.

Don't do it. Non-payment over a prolonged period of time tells you your debtor either can't pay you or won't. Either way, you don't want to waste your time chasing money. Simply call these people and say: "If you don't pay for your old debt, and pay cash for the new work, we won't do any more work for you." Make certain you do this early so you have time to resell the space in your magazine, for example. Don't let deadlines create desperation. Then do as you say. If they don't pay, spend your time selling the space to someone who will pay and who will be a long-term client. You are not in business to be anyone's banker. You are in business to make money. The interest charges you might add to your client's bill will in no way compensate you (or your employee) for the amount of time and postage you will spend trying to collect old debts. The time you spend collecting old debts is time you cannot devote to making sales or managing your company. Collection is an essential part of managing a business that has credit customers. But good management means you extend credit to the credit-worthy — people who will pay you the amount they owe, when they owe it. If you handle collections when you make your sales presentation, your money should arrive in the mail, unless someone brings it to you in person, as promised.

7

SUCCESS

How can you measure success? How will you know when you have it? Success, like salary, is relative to your circumstances and expectations. It is different things to different people. There is personal success; and then there is the type of success that will allow you to stay in business.

Doing a good job is part of personal success. Providing your customers with value, service, and a fair exchange is also a facet of personal success that will foster business success. Business success is measured in dollars and cents. More specifically, it is the money you have left over in the bank after every bill is paid, or "profits." I always considered my personal salary as part of those profits. The IRS seemed to. Whether you pay yourself every month, or wait until the end of the year to see what's left over, as a sole proprietor or partnership, the IRS will tax you on those monies as personal income. So consider what you take home to be a measure of profits, even if your new small business is incorporated. If your business grows and you find yourself with the title Chairman of the Board and you have hired a president to run the corporation, the IRS and SEC will instruct you as to how to measure (and pay taxes on) personal profit (income) and business profit. That is not within the scope of this book.

Add to your salary the amount of cash you have in the bank at the end of the year that is not earmarked to pay ongoing or old debts, to determine your business's profitability.

USING YOUR PROFITS PROFITABLY

What should you do with profits? You should use them to pay your business as well as yourself. Why? Because things change: technology changes, tastes change, your lease agreement may expire and your rent increase or your building be torn down. Your best employee may demand (and deserve) a raise; or he or she might quit and you'll need to train a replacement. Count on change and try to plan for it by having cash in the bank that is not the money you started with, but money the business has earned. Change usually costs money. Some change happens gradually, and the astute business person will keep on top of trends and tastes. But when IBM's engineers announce they have developed the computer that has made yours (and everyone else's) totally obsolete, and that will do more, faster and more cost effectively than anything else that ever existed, someone is going to buy it first and put it to work and start to earn a profit. That someone might as well be you.

Your ability to keep up with (afford to buy and generate profits from) technology and trends is another measure of success. Don't change for change's sake, or only to be first. Make changes if they will make you money or to avoid losing money. My typesetting business depended on an obsolete IBM Composer. It was an odd machine when I started; my competitors had "phototypesetting" equipment. My entire business cost me half the price of a used phototypesetting system. And with my limited technology, I found a market niche. I was able to service customers who needed business stationery, forms, and flyers fast and cheap. The other technology was neither fast nor cheap, but I kept my eye on that technology to see where I stood in the marketplace. At the time, phototypesetting machines were difficult to use, supplies were expensive, and most businesses that used them hired employees to work around the clock to justify their investment.

Then someone (many people) invented desktop publishing software and laser printers. At first, the quality was obviously poor. It did not require an artist's eye to see the ragged edges of letters created from big square dots. But very quickly those dots got smaller and closer together, and I began to see my real competition. Not only was this new technology improving quality fast, but anyone who had ever used a typewriter would learn to use these machines. Phototypesetting equipment required special training and a lot of skill. Desktop publishing was designed for anyone; in fact, for all those people who were coming to me for forms and flyers.

I had set some money aside for the business and invested it in a stat camera. Suddenly, the crystal ball was clear and the bank account empty. The future of my business was in phototypesetting with a modem that could read information transmitted from any office computer. Estimated cost: $20,000 to $50,000. Had I been willing to go into debt, buy new machines, and become an employer, I might have made that choice. I wanted none of those options. Fortunately, I found a buyer who accepted them all.

It's not likely that a business like mine, which generated a total of $18,000 in its fifth year and paid me $10,000 each year, is going to have more than a thousand or two saved in a year. Personally, I could have lived more frugally than I did and saved $5,000, but that was not my choice. Every business owner must make these sorts of choices. The tradeoff is personal success in the early years versus business success in later years. There is no rule; just a choice you have to make. Simply do it with knowledge so you won't be caught by surprise. You may not want to change. Maybe the changes required are not the business you want to be in.

MOVE WITH THE TIMES

Richard Ray Cardall, co-founder of Cardall gift shop, was a customer of mine. He had retired when I met him; his son and granddaughter ran the family business. Richard and his wife had made a nice living selling delicate china figurines, intricate ornaments, and glassware. His descendants carried the same type of merchandise — the type of thing I remember from my grandmother's home. Their market was (literally) dying off. In our fast and busy lives, perhaps we don't have as much time to dust, or as much shelf space to display our treasures as did our grandparents. The Cardalls' clientele was loyal but shrinking. When their mall lease expired and the landlord wanted to raise the rent, they couldn't afford it. Unwilling to change the inventory to suit modern tastes or trends, son Lawrence was forced either to close or relocate. That same year, his father passed away. He chose to move to a new strip mall outside of the downtown area. Time will tell if he made the right choice; my experience indicates that times have changed so much that Cardall gifts will either have to modernize or stop. Loyalty to his father's memory keeps Lawrence Cardall going. He's the first to admit that times are hard. Cardall is hanging on, having invested his profits from a previous business as well as his heart and soul. He talks about wanting his daughter to take over the business; she demonstrates little interest. He has considered selling out.

   I chose not to change; so did Lawrence Cardall. That is all right, but not if you expect to stay in the same business. I gave mine to someone who would, and could afford to, change it. Cardall bemoans his misfortune. My former partner didn't change because he couldn't afford to. It enabled the competition to pass him by.

STAY ON THE EDGE OF TRENDS

Fred Cvar, owner of the Tinder Box, says he'd like to be in the business of selling pipes and tobaccos exclusively. But he knows that is not enough, he says, so he carries gifts. Fred tries to have a gift item in stock first. He visits gift shows twice a year with his spouse, and as soon as other shops display the same merchandise, he finds something else to stock. I used to buy pieces for my collection of clay animals from him. Now I have to shop elsewhere.

But there are more places to buy them. If you are the first and sell out, you will have no competition. You can't do this with service or manufacturing where change requires expensive and time-consuming retooling and/or retraining. But retailers should always strive to be the first and only, then move on ahead of the rest. Service and manufacturing businesses must modernize periodically to remain competitive. Sufficient capital is the key to "success." If you are still making payments on old inventory or equipment, it can be too hard, both monetarily and psychologically, to invest in the new.

One way you can avoid the mad pursuit of selling change is to sell history or tradition. Eric and Betty Gilzean previously owned Betty's Bra Bar and vacationed in Scotland every year. Before they left, friends would ask them to pick up a few things. On every trip, merchants they bought from suggested they take a few extra back to the States. Eventually, demand was so high that it prompted the Gilzeans to open Edinburgh Castle. They sell handknit sweaters, bagpipes, kilts, blouses, plaids, and waistcoats, to name a few. Local and tourist interest in all things Scottish has kept them in business since 1977. Eric says a lot of people who have returned from tours of Scotland discover his shop and buy things from him because they did not find what they wanted, or didn't have enough time to shop, while abroad. The very active Scottish Association in his community provides another source of customers. Several hundred bagpipers in his area need bagpipes and kilts. Highland dancers, both proficient and just-learning, can find kilts, blouses, and velvet waistcoats. For fancy dress balls, says Eric, a Bonnie Prince Charlie Jacket with "jabot" (ruffled bib), a style from the mid-1700s, is very popular attire.

Genealogy, in contrast, became popular with the publication of the book, *Roots*. A lot of people were willing to pay Atheline Wold, owner of Microgen, $10 for a quick search of the family tree. An adequate number of people were interested in family history, internationally, to generate a cottage industry in Salt Lake City, where the world's largest collection of such records is housed in the LDS Church's Family History (Genealogy) Library. Lots of genealogists prospered for about two years after the book became popular, by selling short searches. But more detailed investigation required an investment of $100 or more at a time, payable in advance, with no guarantee that the research would (or could) find any information.

Johni Cerny, owner of Lineages, moved away from marketing the short searches she had done as a subcontractor for Microgen. Her company sells complete, book-bound family histories. Her prices started at $5,000, for which Johni and her staff research the family line as far back in time and as thoroughly as possible, checking not only the Library records, but court, county, and immigration records, diaries, even grave markers, etc.

While Wold continues to market $10 searches and research by the hour, Cerny has built a prosperous business. Wold barely makes a living now. The difference is that Microgen caters to an old fad; Lineages to a long-term market. Microgen made genealogical research affordable for everyone who had read *Roots* and was a little curious. Lineages markets to people who have a genuine interest in family history, who want to leave a complete record for their heirs. Johni also attracts business from serious hobbyists who understand the value of hiring a professional to do extensive research. Lots of other genealogists have either gone out of business or have specialized to cater to the changing market, rather than the fad. In 1988, Atheline returned to Brigham Young University to earn a Master's degree in Norwegian studies, in order to be able to specialize her services.

PAY ATTENTION TO CHANGE

What should a business owner do about change? Simple: pay attention to it. Gain an understanding of why what you are selling sells. And if the reasons change, or the demand changes, change your business. Don't hold onto old ideas or old inventory too long. You can go broke waiting for wide ties and Nehru jackets to come back in style. Don't let your personal feelings about your product line deter you from making changes when the marketplace calls for it. Even *Reader's Digest* magazine contains advertisements, now that subscriptions alone cannot cover production costs.

What they never tell you in business schools is that success or failure is not always in your control. You can start with no capital, manage poorly, and still sell enough to succeed; or you can invest well, manage well, sell a lot, and still fail. Success and failure often depend on circumstances beyond how you operate your business, namely, competition and the economy. If you open the first and only business of its kind and people want to buy your product, you will earn money even if your service is slow and your employees are rude, as long as your pricing is accurate. But when other people copy your idea, or improve upon it, you'll have to whip things into shape. Even after you do, your competitor might have a better location and more up-to-date equipment, simply because he or she entered the marketplace later, with more current information about where to locate and access to new technology.

THE ECONOMY

The national economy is an ever-present danger to any business. When times are good, people feel more comfortable spending money, buying on credit, and catering to perceived needs rather than real needs. With the advent of the latest recession, people affected are spending less. Even for those people who don't suffer any dollar loss or job loss, the effect is psychological — they fear losing their jobs or not getting that next raise.

LOCAL CHANGE

Another factor that can interfere with your success, something you may never consider nor be able to plan for (in most cases) is politics — both business and governmental — as it affects your physical surroundings. I refer to this ever-changing environment as the "local economy." You'll be running your business, attracting customers, putting money in the bank, taking home a substantial paycheck, then all of a sudden, someone will inform you that your block has been slated for redevelopment. You can move or close down. Urban renewal does not happen quickly. If you pay attention, you can anticipate and plan for these changes. Some renewal projects take a more insidious form: mall redevelopment. Since malls are private property, their decisions to remodel are not subject to public hearings. Again, you'll be doing fine and mall management will tell you they don't intend to renew your lease because they're going to tear apart the space you occupy. You may or may not be offered an alternative location in the same mall. Moving will cost you money, in any case.

New business owners have to spend a lot of their time paying attention to day-to-day operations. You may not have time to participate in your town's (or mall's) political process. You should, but if you don't you must prepare for the future by putting money in your bank account for the business. When changes happen, in tastes, in technology, or in your local economy, you can make the choice to change, too, to remain a successful business owner.

8

EXPANSION

If one is profitable, five may make you bankrupt. This principle applies to all types of businesses. Edna's publishing, X-Press Printing (my former partner's company), and Keepsake Jewelry all suffered from the syndrome. The reasons and motivations differed. The end result was the same.

CASE HISTORY #1: TOO MUCH, TOO SOON KILLED THE BUSINESS

Edna's publishing company's original publication, a magazine promoting downtown, was building a loyal readership and a renewing advertising base. However, the sales staff found themselves limited by the amount of advertising space they could sell in a single, monthly, 32-page magazine. So Edna invented a second, in-house, semi-annual magazine and accepted a contract to publish a quarterly mall catalog. The three publications were targeted to specific audiences with a slight overlap in market that allowed successful cross-selling. But the fact that Edna had three magazines instead of one spread working capital very thin. And when the company accepted a contract to do a playbill and another shopping mall catalog, there was little room for failure. Both lost money, and the new catalog competed directly with the company's original downtown magazine; it provided advertisers with an either-or choice and took business away from the company's staple.

In her haste to take on more and more jobs, each of which depended on advertising sales to pay for production, Edna neglected the fact that the company's retention rate for salespeople was two — including herself. Not only was working capital spread thin, her time was as well. The company's monthly magazine nearly died of neglect. New salespeople could only comprehend — and sell — each upcoming publication. Edna created a third company magazine. After one period in which the business produced five magazines in about five weeks, the monthly was cut to twenty-four pages, simply because no one had the time to sell it. Health and legal problems further diluted the owner's time. When Edna examined the bottom line, she was unable to give the pay raises she had anticipated, and company morale dropped to nothing. Her three salaried employees began to job hunt; she had to hire and train salespeople once every two or three weeks after the last batch left in discouragement.

CASE HISTORY #2: RELYING ON NONEXISTENT INVESTMENTS FOR EXPANSION

John Felt's Heritage Keepsake Diamonds' story was a bit different. After running one store in Utah successfully for a number of years, John said a number of investors convinced him to open fourteen more stores all over the western part of the U.S. John found himself expanding the business faster than he could personally control and taking on a great amount of debt to do so. As the national economy worsened in the early '80s, and the bank loans began to eat up the profits, John turned to his partners to produce the cash investments they had promised, only to find out that the money never existed. He sold ten stores, keeping five in Utah and Idaho, and tried to recover. Twenty percent and higher interest rates in a business that required purchasing inventory on credit put him into Chapter 11 bankruptcy. Eventually, John sold the business, but new management failed to save it.

CASE HISTORY #3: EXPANSION FOR THE WRONG REASONS

Fred Blackburn's story of business success and then failure is very complex. He successfully operated a PIP quick printing franchise for a decade. When a downtown renovation eliminated most of the parking near his business and made access difficult, sales began to decline. He lost his franchise and continued to operate as Fred's X-Press Printing. A few years later, Fred was evicted from his downtown location — the building had been sold and was going to be torn down and replaced with a new bank office tower. Wanting to keep both a mall presence and a downtown store, he chose to move across the street into another new building. Moving was not new to Fred; he had had to do it twice before. But this time he had to pay for plumbing, wiring, and interior wall construction — and business was bad. Furthermore, quick print shops were proliferating in the downtown area at the time. And photocopy businesses using high quality, high speed machines further eroded his market share. Nevertheless, after Fred moved, he found himself with an extra printing press that didn't fit into his tiny new shop. So he decided to open a third store, just because he had the equipment, he said, even though he did not have enough equipment to open a full-service shop or enough capital to upgrade his own photocopying machines. He was saved from bankruptcy by a buyer, who closed the third location immediately.

THE MORAL OF THE STORY

Go slow if you decide to expand. More isn't better unless more meets the same criteria as the first: there is market demand and you make money. Clair and Twila Hale owned two Hallmark shops in one mall and a third in the mall across the street. The demand for greeting cards and seasonal gifts is strong; their ability to carry an inventory of popular and constantly changing gifts has enabled them to keep up with market demand and, essentially, become their own competition. In response to a recent mall renovation, the Hales moved one of their two shops into a third shopping center five miles away.

Carriage Horse Livery's president, Wayne Scott, started his business with two horses and two reproduction carriages. The company grew to 10 carriages, 18 to 20 horses, 2 hay wagons, a sleigh, and a horse-drawn trolley. Wayne said ten carriages is all that the city can support. However, another company competes with his. Still, he realizes that for the hours and demand he anticipated in a city the size of Salt Lake, he has enough. His "enough" was based on being the only such business in the city; competition may change the statistics. Competition also prompted him to start advertising, which may increase demand in his favor.

Carrie expanded Body Tech as needed. When her classes grew too large to fit in her basement, she signed a lease agreement and opened a studio. She leased more space as her business grew, but kept her flight attendant job for security, so she could always meet the lease payments. After eight years, Carrie had a studio custom designed in a new office building near downtown. Rather than add new studios, which would dilute her time and attention, Carrie works from her large office in her single studio and finds ways to use her time more productively. She produced a workout video and book. She says about the increased competition in the aerobics business, "My theory is, they've caught up, so leave them behind and come up with something new."

CAN YOU AFFORD TO EXPAND?

Make certain you can afford to expand. Don't expand on promises or the expectation that someone else is going to invest. People invest in assets and profits, not in liabilities and plans. You'll probably have to spend your own money, which can include a bank or private loan. But you have to pay back loans, so it is still your money.

Also consider your staff. If you ask your employees to take on more projects, like Edna's publishing company, can you increase their salaries? Are their salaries sufficiently high for you to expect more work for the same pay? Ask them what they think. If the publishing company had found an adequate number of salespeople, perhaps it could have worked. But it did not, and it would have made more sense to take on new projects after a sales force had been developed than to hire a batch of new people who were trying to learn not only sales techniques but a new product line a week before press deadline.

BE REALISTIC

Body Tech not only had enough customers to justify expansion, it had a loyal, dependable, eager cadre of instructors who also viewed expansion as an opportunity.

If you do expand too much or too soon, have the wisdom to retrench. At one time the Hales owned seven Hallmark stores some fifty miles apart. Even though two sons and one daughter helped run the business, the family decided seven stores were too many to operate well, so they sold three. In October of 1986, opportunity and "a new challenge" called once again and the Hales opened The Christmas Store in the same mall as their first two Hallmark stores (Clair's Hallmark and Twila's Hallmark). But after the holidays, they closed the location, choosing not to renew their temporary lease. The experiment did not justify a year-round Christmas store.

Mike Mihlberger expanded Office & Things from its single Salt Lake location to a second store in Oklahoma. He says, "I went to Oklahoma to look for a wife." He met and married a Utah woman, closed the Tulsa store after tiring of the commute, and concentrated his expansion activities in Utah. At first, Mike sold specialty gifts as well as business supplies and typewriters. Later, Mike expanded his gift line and opened another store in the mall across the street. As his family grew from two to four, his interests changed. "I needed toys at wholesale for my kids." He re-examined his marketing strategy. "The only toy a kid remembers is a stuffed animal." Mike closed his second mall store and eliminated his giftware line because it overlapped the inventory of the store across the hall from his primary location. He put an extensive line of stuffed animals in the extra space. He calls his stuffed animal store "Noah's Ark" and specializes in collectibles. His decision to open a bakery next door was motivated similarly. "My family was growing, I needed to buy food wholesale." The other (maybe the real) reason was the bakery in his mall closed, so he thought there would be a continued demand. He also decided to alter the bakery-business' standard means of operation.

Rather than have a baker work on site, he simply buys wholesale from bakers all over town. The products are as fresh; the variety infinite. His expansions have always been in response to market demand, not optimism or wishful thinking. And when demand changes, or competition increases, he's willing to adjust the nature of his business. Mike has been in business since 1975, and he had a loyal staff of people who don't mind selling $3,000 pens one day and 50 cent breakfast rolls the next. He expanded with both sufficient capital and the agreement of his existing staff, one of whom said the change of pace keeps the job interesting.

BUSINESS MUST BE PROFITABLE

Remember, business should be profitable. You will have a lot more work to do in the early years when you have to run your business all the time. Be careful not to inflict unnecessary stress on yourself by taking on more than you, your funds, and your staff can handle. If you create a successful business, you'll have plenty of time to "do more." In the early years, building a clientele, training and building a loyal staff, and building a capital reserve should be your priorities. Why? Because if these go badly, they will threaten the survival of your business. Accomplishing these things will take a lot of your time, attention, and money in the first five years.

You'll advertise to attract attention and to generate word-of-mouth publicity. This costs more in the first few years because when you are new you have to pay for exposure; the free stuff comes later. If you ask other people (your employees) to "hook their wagons to your star," you have to be there for them as well as for the business. You have to be visible. Having worked for three start-up companies (including my own), I know it is hard to stay loyal to a company or a boss who is not constantly involved in the operation of his or her own business. I've seen coworkers start to lose their morale and put forth less effort to make sales or service customers, because the owner started to take a lot of time off for vacations, or even to operate a second or third location. Since the business was new, the owner delegated far more responsibility than authority, and when problems arose, employees were left hanging — unable to solve the problem, please the customer, or do their jobs. Working under these conditions is miserable. You will need to be in the office or store more than you think, just to serve as a role model — if the boss works hard, employees will believe that the company is going to succeed. If the boss is never around, employees start to worry that things are going wrong, otherwise why would the boss be so hard to find? Don't rush into other ventures until your staff is well-trained, and has gained your trust, so that you can hand them not only the keys to the door, but the authority and knowledge to handle whatever happens in your absence immediately. Sound simple? It is, but you won't do it for a year or two. It's just not comfortable for either you, the owner, or for your employees.

CHECK YOUR SAVINGS

Finally, before you expand, consider the amount of cash you have in the bank. Not the money you or others invested when you got started, or your working capital, but your savings. Odds are by the time you actually opened for business you didn't have much start-up capital left. If you did, add to it as though you were saving for retirement and you had been guaranteed that Social Security will not exist and you will live to be 100. Save regularly and as much as you can. "Savings" are monies that you do not pay to yourself, the owner. Having this money demands that you have the self-discipline to pay yourself last — after the bills, the staff, the savings account, taxes, and whatever else happens.

YOUR ABILITY TO GROW DEPENDS ON MONEY

In the first one to five years, pay yourself very little, because your ability to grow depends on how much money you have in the bank. Lending institutions are more willing to loan money to people who will risk (that's risk *losing*) money of their own. Your goal is to have so much money saved that you can either pay cash for expansion or attract loans that you know you will be able to pay off, whatever happens, because you have the cash flow and money in the bank.

Sheri and Jay Jensen manufacture and market the Jensen ThermoShield — a quilted waterbed cover that eliminates the need to heat a waterbed electrically. Sheri invented the ThermoShield in 1982 because the family couldn't afford their electric bills. Originally, they turned their basement into a manufacturing plant. Along with their five children, Sheri and Jay cut pads, hemmed fabric, and sewed straps. For three years, Sheri made phone calls and set appointments; after work, Jay made sales calls in people's homes.

The Jensens lived modestly and put most of their profit back into the business. Jay began to sell his product at state and county fairs, shopping mall shows, and home and garden shows in 1985. That first year, working full-time, he earned $20,000, more than he had ever earned as an employee. The Jensens now pay themselves $125,000 and still reinvest most of their income into the business.

Jensen ThermoShield was five years old when the Jensens took out their first loan. They did so to buy a quilting machine and build a garage-factory on their lot in Riverton, Utah, explains Jay, because the mattress factory they subcontracted to could not keep up with demand. Furthermore, the monthly payments on the loan were the same amount as they had paid the subcontractor.

While I doubt many businesses operate this way, they should. The ones that do, like the Hales and the Jensens, are the first to expand in response to market demand. They are the ones that survive economic changes — fiscal or political — like recessions, stock market crashes, fluctuating interest rates, perhaps even urban (or mall) renewal projects. They have the money to move, to buy new inventory, to upgrade their equipment, to train their staff. It is all right to compete with yourself if doing so will increase your overall profitability. But if adding a new store across the street means people will no longer shop at your first location (or buy ads in your monthly magazine), it's not a good idea.

HAVE THE SUPPORT OF YOUR STAFF

Consider the support of your staff before you want to grow. If you operate more than one store, you will have to be in different places during the day. You will have to be able to count on your best people to manage for you, as you would. Asking them to do more on the same pay because all your capital will be used for expansion is not reasonable. You probably paid them less than they were worth when you started your business; they accepted that because they expected to earn a great deal more as the business earned more. You are going to make those people mad at you if you use profits to expand before you increase their salaries.

Of course, if your employees have no skills and require none, this is not an issue. But even minimum wage, low skill employees can offer your business ingredients for success that may make their happiness a bigger priority than expansion. For instance, if your clerk always smiles and remembers regular customers by name, always takes the correct payment and gives the right change, you'd be foolish to think that employee is easily replaceable.

Highly skilled or low on skills, people can, in fact, be replaced. But it will take new people time to learn your business procedures. If you have to train new people in the middle of an expansion, you are going to have a difficult time. Why not wait until your employees feel well paid, dedicated, and willing to *assist* you with your expansion. What's the rush to get bigger? Are you afraid your competitor will do it first? Could be, but so what. Doing it first only counts if you can do it well and *keep doing it.* First doesn't count if your valued employees quit and your company goes broke because you don't have the time to train their replacements. Let someone else be "first" under those conditions. When they quit, pick up their customers.

If you sell gifts, you should always try to be first. But gifts change constantly. So whenever you enter the market, you have an opportunity to sell "the new." But if you plan to publish a monthly magazine, once you start it is a mistake to tell people who signed contracts and paid their deposits for upcoming issues that you changed your mind and want to take a few months off. They probably won't do business with you again, judging from the history of one local publication.

Be realistic. Examine all the factors. Don't react to the competition; make sound business decisions and let competitors react to you.

9

MAKING MONEY

No one is in business to create jobs or pay taxes. No one. Real entrepreneurs take the risks they do to make money. The paychecks their employees draw every month, and the wide variety of goods and services American consumers have to select from, are all byproducts.

The extent to which the American public has come to believe (and insist) that the opposite is true may confuse the new business owner. And it is highly likely that in the early years, paying taxes and creating jobs will be more of what you do than make money for yourself.

WHAT DO YOU PAY YOURSELF?

How will you know how much to pay yourself? In the early years the formula is simple: what's left over, after you pay debts, taxes, salaries, and the company's investment capital fund. What is left over for you to take home is going to depend on: how much you sell, how much you spend to stay in business, and what prices you charge. Beginners tend to spend too much and charge too little. Furthermore, service businesses often neglect to charge for "real time." How much you sell will be determined by market demand, how well you let the market know you exist, the competition, your location, the national and local economy, and a hundred other things, about half of which you can control.

WHAT DO YOU CHARGE?

In my business, I sold "typesetting." I decided that I would charge my clients from the time my fingers touched the keyboard of my machine, to the moment I had the finished piece pasted up. What I did not charge for was the five minutes or two days that I designed in my head. How could I, I thought to myself, charge anyone for something as abstract as "thinking."

That was a mistake. I learned from experience that charging for thinking is not only fair but *necessary*. Perhaps other people designed logos with pen and paper or computer. The fact that I "saw" logos in my head was no less legitimate and should have been income-producing from the beginning, rather than two years later. When I wrote ads for Edna's, I started the time clock from the moment I began the project to when the finished copy left the typewriter (or computer). I charged for all that time I spent listening to my head talk. That's what I had been hired to do. My employer defined what "time" we were to charge for.

Had I charged for my creativity as owner of Midnight Oil Typesetting, I might have been more successful. I also had to decide how much to charge. Since I had a six month record of pricing and income, it was fairly simple to do. The going rate in the business when I started was $25 an hour. Since my machine was low-end, I set my price at $20. I calculated that if I did an hour of billable work a day, I could cover my overhead. I knew with Fred's X-Press Printing as my only customer, I would do more.

Consider the Competition

Setting prices relative to the competition is a good place to start. But make certain that you will cover your expenses. There are a lot of low bidders out there who are courting bankruptcy. Be careful not to copy them. Set your prices realistically higher. Justify the difference with quality and service. Then let others copy you.

You should charge as much as people are willing to pay. Is it better to sell five for $20 each or ten for $10? Well, the cost of your inventory for five will be lower, but people will like you better if you charge $10. If each item costs you $7, you're going to make more selling fewer for a higher price. However, if a customer comes to your store for that particular item and you've run out, he or she may think that you don't have much to offer and may never come back. What should you do if purchasing 100 at a time will only cost you $5 each?

Your prices must balance your need to attract customers and your need to afford an ample inventory. Naturally, the type of item you sell will help you decide both. If you sell custom-made roll-top desks, like Charlie, you don't have to carry any inventory of finished goods, just floor samples. You can order supplies when you need them and charge as much as the traffic will bear. If you sell jewelry, like Guy, one or two of a kind will do. Since you can always size a ring, your customers will be more attracted by a large variety. If you are in the grocery business, you need fully stocked shelves so that customers will find everything they need, every time they come into your place of business, or they will have to go elsewhere. In clothing retail, you need a variety of styles as well as sizes at the beginning of each selling season. You need a big selection so that as sizes and styles start to sell out, customers have plenty to choose from until the next season's merchandise arrives. When the selection is very thin, and the new inventory is due to arrive soon, it's time for clearance sales.

As you can see, experience in one's profession will give you a head start when you buy inventory and set prices. It will take a year or two on your own before you have records upon which to base such decisions. Generally speaking, if you cater to immediate needs ("real need") you have to have an ample inventory at the "best" price. If you cater to "perceived needs," a wide variety of ever-changing merchandise will attract customers. Your prices will depend on your costs of doing business and the quality and service you offer.

BUSINESS SPENDING

Not only do small business owners tend to charge too little, they often think they have to spend too much to stay in business. Sometimes finding out what "too much" is, is a matter of trial and error. But you have to pay attention. Spending too much is often necessary as long as it doesn't happen for too long a period of time. Advertising is going to cost a lot in the beginning, simply because you need the exposure, unless you want to wait five years for word-of-mouth to build your business. The mistake entrepreneurs often make is they buy too much advertising, all at once, run out of money, then discontinue advertising completely — because "they can't afford it."

You Can't Afford Not to Advertise

You probably can't afford not to. But you need to find out what you can afford to do that will be effective. So contact every publication in your area and find out whom they target. If you intend to attract customers from an entire metropolitan area, the newspaper will reach that market. If you want to sell to college students, the school paper or local arts and entertainment tabloids are right. How about the entire state? Perhaps yours has a regional magazine? The nation? Define your market more specifically: businesses, households, sports enthusiasts, and do some research.

Collect rate sheets and information on each publication's circulation. Surveys indicate that about four people read every copy of a magazine, and publishers like to use this statistic. If a magazine claims 40,000 "readers," they probably print 10,000. You can bet they keep 500 in the office for the salespeople to use, and perhaps another one percent of their print run is left over at the end of the month, undistributed and unread. So ask for press run figures and compare those.

More important, find out where those copies go. Is the publication distributed for free, mailed to paid subscribers, and/or available on the newsstand? If you have a gift shop in the downtown area, and the regional magazine is mailed to subscribers all over the state, just how many reach your target market? Ask. Is there a magazine or newspaper that is distributed to the workers and tourists in your area exclusively? Maybe they print fewer copies; but if the copies are hand delivered to your potential customers, it could be a better buy.

Targeting Your Advertising

I said "could be" because these issues are never that black and white. Most likely you will find two or three publications you'd like to try. Here's the rule: try them one at a time. Reread the chapter about how advertising works. In summary, it is an image builder. Remember that restaurant it took us five years to get around to trying? That's to be expected. So how can you tell if an ad is effective? You have to be patient and methodical. If you have narrowed the field to targeted publications, set an advertising budget, and had an effective ad designed, then place your ad in your first choice for at least six months. Don't think a 10% off coupon on a $200 item (or even a $20 item) is going to make people flock to your store. Be realistic. If you sell fast food, half-off and two-for-one coupons are likely to create some traffic, if people read that magazine or newspaper.

Coupons are effective for inexpensive or frequently used items, like food or household cleaning products. Display advertising works best for retailers and service businesses that want to build name recognition and a customer base. Feature a single item in your display ad, along with a memorable logo and a unique look designed to catch attention. The featured item might also have a "special price." Gauge the reaction to your ad by keeping track of how many featured items you sell before and after you run the ad. Content (copywriting) and design (artwork and layout) work together to make an ad effective. A professional can help here. Not everyone who works at an ad agency is highly skilled. Find someone who is, who has a track record; then spend part of your advertising budget to have an effective ad (or series of similar ads) designed. Use your "look" consistently to build name recognition and an image.

After a six-month period, place an ad in your second choice publication for the same time period. When you find out which publication is most effective, judging by the sales figures, stick with it (or them). Be consistent until years have passed and you have so much business you don't want to handle any more. Then run an occasional ad so that old customers are reminded of your existence. Invisibility implies nonexistence. You should also build a mailing list. Every time you sell something, try to get a name and address. If you use sales contracts or hand-written sales receipts, this is easy to do. Another way to build a mailing list is to collect business cards. Have a drawing, for example; put a fishbowl on your counter for cards and give away something small — an excellent idea for restaurants. Edna's publishing company has a monthly business card drawing and a trivia contest. Magazine readers answer questions based on ads and articles in her downtown magazine. Prizes are typically donated in exchange for free publicity in the magazine. Classy Lady's Judy Harris uses her mailing list to announce the arrival of each season's inventory, and she has found her response rate is higher from direct mail than any other form of advertising. But direct mail to a mailing list only reaches existing customers. So don't limit yourself. Put a "guest register" and pen on your counter. How about television? It reaches everyone. Are you selling to everyone? Mr. Mac clothing store does. They have one of the largest inventories of men's suits in the state, and stores statewide. They want to reach the "mass market." Mac uses television and newspaper almost exclusively. They work for his business.

Radio is similar to print. These days at least one radio station exists for every taste. In most cities where thousands of people are captive audiences on freeways and highways every morning and evening, radio allows you to target your market. Treat it just like publications. Get the prices, the demographics (who listens, what they earn, where they shop), and try each station that targets your market, one at a time.

Check the Competition

Pay attention to what the competition is doing with their advertising. Just as jewelry and shoe stores tend to flock together in shopping malls, so do their ads in newspapers and magazines. Then there is Tiffany's and its image equivalent in Salt Lake, O.C. Tanner. Those ads are on the backs of Playbills. Plan your advertising the same way you plan the location of your business. Are you catering to people who will shop around, or is your product so special that they'll seek you out? Who are "they"? Put your advertising dollars in the medium that "they" read, watch, or listen to. You will be amazed at the quantity of data that advertising salespeople will give you. Take all that information, and your personal knowledge of who buys what you are trying to sell, and target your ads to those people.

Be patient, be consistent, don't hang on to one choice because you like the salesperson or even the radio station. After a trial period, look at your own numbers.

DON'T LOOK FOR TOO MUCH INCOME IMMEDIATELY

Too many people try to make a living from their businesses right away. They pay themselves the salary they made at their last jobs, or some sum they think they are "worth," and go broke. Again, your cost of doing business will be higher in the first few years. You'll have to buy more, pay cash for your supplies and inventory, and take home less. It will take a year or two before you build a line of credit. Even so, you should never get into more debt than you can afford to pay in your worst month. Some business owners talk their suppliers into letting them pay over time. This is only wise if you can make the payments. But if your credit customers are slow to pay you, or your sales don't meet your projections, how are you going to pay your suppliers?

Consider your salary to be a "debt" the company must pay. Then pay yourself, like all debts, as much as the company can afford in a worst month, and pay your debt to yourself last. When you start, your salary should be conservatively low, based on your income projections. After your first year, you will know what your worst month really is. (In retail, it's usually January and March. In service, December.) Don't assume that next year sales will increase, so you can pay yourself more. Wait until sales do increase, in fact. Live as frugally as possible until the business can afford to pay you and your staff more. If reality exceeds your projections, give yourself a bonus on December 31st, after you have calculated your net profits for the year. Since the IRS is going to tax you, as a sole proprietor or a partnership, on what's left over anyway, this is the time to pay the business (capital) and pay yourself that bonus.

TAKE TIME TO REASSESS

January 1st is a good time to look into the future, too. What is changing in your world? What will it cost you to buy updated equipment or the latest giftware inventory? Of course, income you have earned from sales all year long has bought new inventory and supplies. But what if times have changed dramatically, and you have to buy something that will enable you to continue to compete in the marketplace — like the phototypesetting machines that kept Midnight Oil Typesetting in business. Or you have a large inventory of your best selling pink ceramic flamingos; and no one is buying them. You still have to buy new inventory and either discount those flamingos or put them in storage for another decade.

Then take home what's left over. Does it sound like you are going to work for free for a few years? It is possible. Some people do, or they make half as much as they could earn if they had a salaried job.

Why? Because if you survive the first five years, it's likely you will be able to make more than you could ever earn working for someone else. That is — that should be — why you started a business. There are more reasons to start a business, which I'll discuss in a later chapter. But making money is what will keep you in business and allow you to fulfill those other goals and needs. It is also the only thing that will justify all the hard work you must do to succeed.

AVOID DEBT

Getting into debt in the early years is not advisable. Your company will have a greater chance of surviving for a longer period of time if you don't owe anyone any money. It is simple to skip paying yourself a salary one month. Try skipping payment on a loan or a payable. You'll find yourself spending a lot of time on the telephone with creditors. This will interfere with everything else you need to do to make your business succeed. It will take up your time, will exhaust your mental and physical energy, and could cost you money — in interest payments or attorney's fees. If you aren't sleeping nights because you owe money, you won't make good business decisions. You'll be too tired, for one thing, too desperate for another. You might start lying, then you'll start to believe those lies and begin to operate your business based on "fending off creditors" rather than "attracting customers." I've seen it happen many times. The type of debt I'm talking about is not the money you have to spend to buy inventory and supplies for the day-to-day operation of your business ("working capital"). It is long-term loans from banks and lenders, or lines of credit you have taken advantage of (abused) beyond any reasonable expectation that you can actually afford to pay the debt. Reasonable expectation is what you can afford in a poor month, based on actual sales and expense figures. Going beyond that means you have projected that business is going to get better. It should, and you should project it, but only on paper as a personal goal for you and your staff. Don't get into debt based on those projections. Get into debt in direct proportion to your ability to pay.

Some new business owners break these rules. They find investors and loans and somehow or another sell the one product that the world has been waiting for. If you have one of those, you'll have to take the risk. If you're like most of us, think twice.

TRADE AND BARTER

A word about trade. Trade is not money except to the IRS. You have to pay taxes on the market value of anything you take in trade. You have to pay cash when you have not received cash. Can you afford to do this? If your company operates on a shoestring, where do you expect to get this tax money from?

Don't trade working capital, only "excess profit." New companies almost never have excess profits. Unless you start your business on the large sum of working capital your family gave you, or the money you earned from your last successful business, like the Gilzeans' Edinburgh Castle, you are probably cash short. Remember, you have to build a cash reserve for the business; and, chances are, in the first year both you and your employees are grossly underpaid. You need cash to pay for everything.

Years from now, you'll have a track record and some savvy. Your inventory purchases more closely match demand. You sell almost everything you buy at retail, and keep up with market trends, economic conditions, and changing times. You've given yourself and your staff frequent and substantial pay raises. Your employees are telling you they want to work for you until they retire because their salaries are so high and they have good health and retirement benefits. You have trained a trustworthy and dedicated manager and can finally take a vacation. And for the first time, your profits exceed all your projections and expectations. After you pay your bills, salaries, taxes, and business, and yourself, you discover you still have a bunch of cash in the bank that you have no foreseeable use for. This is "excess profit." Coincidentally, you try to sell an ad to a company that rents time-share condos in Hawaii. They will only accept trade. You've got the cash to pay taxes, and you were planning to vacation in Hawaii in a hotel that would have cost the same as the time-share condo. These are the conditions under which to accept trade.

You may be very tempted to take trade for things you don't need just to get customers in the start-up years. Big mistake. For one thing, trade won't pay your bills. Remember, I said pay yourself *last*. When you accept trade, you pay yourself first. Trading may cause you to run short of cash to pay debts because your creditors won't accept pass-along trade. Your staff will start to wonder why you can afford a new wardrobe, a new car, and luxurious vacations when their salaries are so small. They will resent you; morale will plummet.

Consider one other negative aspect of trade you will have to live with: once a customer has traded, he or she will expect to do so forever. Just how many meals in restaurants, overnight stays at local hotels, and gold necklaces do you need? How much can you really use? You'll find that your trade certificates start to pile up in your desk drawer. You can't use all those ballet tickets, and the season is almost over. After you give five away to your employees, a nice bonus, you'll throw away three that no one can use. Now you have lost money. And the people who traded with you were hoping you would, because your loss was their gain. They had excess profits. They only traded for things they really needed and could use right away. They did not need the cash to stay in business.

Taking trade is a vicious cycle; one that is almost impossible to break. Just try telling a customer who is acclimated to trading that he or she has to pay cash. He or she will not believe you. Odds are, you will not do business with that customer for a long, long time.

If you continue to ask for cash, and don't back down at the last minute (which is a bitter temptation for a publisher whose magazine has to go to press whether the space is filled or not), perhaps those people will agree to do business with you in the future for money.

As an employee, the most annoying thing an employer ever did to me was to do business in trade. Employers like to pretend that trade doesn't count. I consider it salary. So when my boss complained that she "took no money home," while she modeled her fur coat and her jewels, my stomach turned. Our initial staff of three had agreed to income goals for us all when we started. To me it looked like she was not only getting paid, but getting more than her share of what we had all contributed to. We had all worked equally hard to create a successful company; the cash value of her trade was five times my monthly salary. I do believe an employer is entitled to more than an employee. But her denial that she was getting paid at all led me to believe that her willingness to pay me more had dropped to zero. In fact, it had at the time. She could only see her lack of cash in proportion to our cash salaries. It was a real morale killer for the company.

She never took our advice to stop trading (our advice was free). It took the advice of a paid CPA to tell her she was courting disaster. She slowed down but didn't stop. Edna did business with a lot of the same organizations I used to. They paid me cash when I said "no" to trade. If you are tempted to trade, there is one exception to the rule: trade for essential supplies. For example, if you are a printer, it's all right to trade printing for paper and ink. Trade only for things that you can use in your business, which will, in turn, produce income and profit. If you trade inventory (i.e., an item from your line of gifts) for anything, put that thing on display for sale.

Just remember, nine out of ten new businesses fail in the first year. Half of those remaining will be gone five years later. Why? A lot of reasons, but poor management and lack of capital summarize most of them.

THE ENTREPRENEURIAL SPIRIT

Why work that hard for an uncertain income and future? Because you are an entrepreneur. Because you want to, and it is important to you to take that risk. If you take the risk well, you'll have things that money cannot buy. My favorite was control of my time. I set my store hours and days off. I worked late when necessary and left early when business was seasonally slow. But I was always promoting. Everyone I met knew me as a business owner. Something about that felt important to me. (I miss it now, which is why I freelance write.) If you have that type of personality, you have no choice. You will start a business. Most small business owners make a comfortable living for themselves and their families if they succeed. Dreams of six-month vacations die hard. Ask a small business owner about taking time off. Most will answer that they don't. The living that most make is better than a salaried job, if you count the "benefits." But the store always needs minding. That is how they keep it going long enough for the kids to take it over.

AN ENTREPRENEURIAL PERSONALITY

How can you tell if you have an entreprencurial personality? You have to be honest with yourself about yourself.

There are two categories of workers: the Risk Takers and the Security Seekers. Risk takers are potential business owners. Security seekers are perfect employees.

ARE YOU A RISK TAKER OR A SECURITY SEEKER?

Security seekers are the type of people who live for the weekend. They do a job for the paycheck and find comfort in becoming skilled at a specific job or trade. They like working for companies with long histories — a sign that they can count on having a job as long as they choose. Some security seekers are manager material; others will never get out of the mailroom. But none of them want to take work home on the weekends.

Risk takers like change and challenges. They want to be in charge of their lives — make decisions about what they do and how they do it. These people are willing to take both credit and blame for their actions. There are corporate-type risk takers, who, given the capital and laboratory facilities, will invent new products and technologies, perhaps create a subsidiary company. And there are entrepreneurial risk takers; they want to own the fruits of their ingenuity. Risk takers carry their jobs around with them all the time. Even if they aren't doing work at home, they are thinking about it — what needs doing Monday — or planning some new project.

In addition to being risk takers, the entrepreneurs I have met and interviewed (myself included) possess another characteristic that seems universal — they don't "fit in" and they don't want to fit in. These people are not the "dress for success" crowd. They don't enjoy making friends and influencing people to achieve promotions up the corporate ladder. I think the real entrepreneur is, above all else, open and honest.

Not everyone who owns a business at any given moment has an entrepreneurial personality. Those who do, start businesses to enable themselves to earn an honest living, perhaps for the rest of their lives.

Entrepreneurs realize that while clothing may project some sort of image, it has absolutely nothing to do with running a business. A tailored suit may help you if you work in the capacity of salesperson for your own company. But behind the scenes, in the offices, it is more important to be comfortable. Being comfortable lets your mind work. Entrepreneurs are comfortable — they are easy to be around and are self-assured.

Unlike security seekers, risk-taker entrepreneurs integrate "job" into their personality. They see themselves in terms of what they do for a living; they have a great deal of ego investment in their work. When one is that ego-involved, it is hard to trust one's fate to another person. Running things, knowing that success and failure are your challenge and responsibility, becomes the only choice.

Real entrepreneurs like to do business based on old values of honesty and trust — "business on a handshake." Most suffer from too much trust in other people, who may not have entrepreneurial personalities.

An entrepreneur has the ability to motivate the overworked and the underpaid. Entrepreneurs are leaders. They have the ability to get other people to agree to their dreams and help them achieve success. Why? Because a real entrepreneur is a good communicator. Management is like marriage: you have to be able to tell people you work with what is going on so that they agree to help you accomplish mutual goals.

Entrepreneurs tend to stay that way for life. Which might explain why prospective employers wanted documentation on my previous three employers rather than my client list, after I had sold my company. My previous employers had all gone out of business. But maybe the prospective employers were accurate in assuming that a former business owner would have a hard time taking orders. It is true. For a time, I had a job in which I could control my work schedule. I had a "partnership" working relationship with my employer. When I lost that relationship, it became especially difficult to go to work in the morning. Deep down, I still want to work for myself.

That also might explain why so many business owners, who are now running successful companies, at one time or another owned a business that failed. Does it sound like an entrepreneur must be self-sacrificing? I believe that to be true.

Some people start businesses with the intent to pay only themselves. They do not pay their suppliers and they keep employees in the perpetual poorhouse. Some get rich at the expense of everyone they've done business with; some go bankrupt, some to jail. They are not real entrepreneurs. But let's not dwell on the dishonest people. Let's take a closer look at the characteristics of those who are in business to stay.

OTHER ENTREPRENEURIAL CHARACTERISTICS

Another observation I have made about people who start businesses is they tend to be either young (twenty-one to thirty) or unemployed at the time. Perhaps it is because young people don't have as many financial obligations or expectations about how much they should earn. Whatever income they produce from running their small business is, for a time, enough. The unemployed also have little to lose. People who work for large corporations at exorbitant salaries with company-sponsored pension plans simply have too much to lose. Would I advise someone making $50,000 a year, with insurance and pension benefits, to risk small business? Not a chance. Certainly the upside potential is higher than that. But the risk of failure is higher still.

If you are comfortable with what you do for a living, stick with it. But if the job you go to each morning makes you dread the morning alarm, then save a big chunk of that salary each year until you have enough to live on for a year or two in the style to which you have grown accustomed, plus some capital for the company to grow on. You will have an advantage over the rest of the pack with money in the bank. But don't start a business that is completely out of your field of expertise. If something novel interests you, start on a part-time basis. Can the business be run with a full-time manager other than yourself? Perhaps another member of your family (husband, wife, grown children) can run the business full-time while you phase out of permanent employment. Work on the weekends and evenings to develop your skills. Then "retire" into a business of your own, as Bev Miller did, the woman who bought Midnight Oil Typesetting from me. As public relations director for a state agency, she often had to have pamphlets published. She gained an understanding of the typesetting business from the other side of the counter — as a customer. Learning the machinery was simple enough; and her daughter(s) ran the business until she left her state job.

Entrepreneurs just don't like to work for someone else. Why? Because they would prefer to work for the best and smartest boss they know — themselves. Everyone else is an unknown. I'm never confident that an employer will run his or her company well. It makes me uncomfortable to be a potential victim of someone else's inability to make intelligent, informed, accurate business decisions. And I have no way of knowing which is the case. As a business owner, or a writer, I have a sense of control over the outcome, a greater willingness to live with the consequences of my own decisions.

People do change. And while owners of new businesses tend to fit the profile I have described, those who have been at it for a number of years may behave differently. After years of coping with the reality of running a business — meeting payroll, spending long hours filling out forms, having people who owe you money treat you like a loan shark — people change. Some of the humble and lovable features wear off. Some of the shyness does too. It is hard to sell other people on your dreams if you are shy. You have to do public relations for your own company all the time. Everyone you meet should leave the encounter knowing your name and the name of your company and what you sell. You have to be a walking, talking billboard — maybe forever. This will change you, too.

Finally, the two things that change the small business owner the most are success and failure. Almost everyone experiences a little of both. But after five years, you'll know which category your business falls into, and you will have been changed by the process. The successful will want more time to themselves. Time becomes a precious commodity for the successful entrepreneur. The unsuccessful will change in ways that they could never have imagined (nor could their family or friends). If you fail gracefully — pay your debts and quit — you will be sad, and ready to do it better the next time. If you fail miserably — go bankrupt and leave debts unpaid — you will have also lost some of your honesty along with your business. Don't believe it? I have come to believe that this is a psychological self-defense mechanism. Healthy for the individual in the short run; disastrous for the business and all your future endeavors.

WRAPPING IT UP

It is perfectly acceptable to close your business. Not every good idea is a good business. Not everyone who starts a business should have done so. After sixty years, some people want to retire, can't find a buyer, don't have any offspring who want to run the business, so they just stop. Simply pay attention to your profit and loss statements and your gut feelings, so you can guide your company into a long and prosperous future, or end it gracefully and try some other way to make a living (another venture or employment).

If you truly have an entrepreneurial personality — you are a risk taker — then you'll keep trying. Not always right away. After all, economic conditions may not be just right, yet. Be patient with yourself, and try to time every venture to catch the next wave of worldwide economic prosperity. In retail, open in time for the Christmas shopping season.

11

IT'S ALL IN HOW YOU SELL

Now that you know what to sell, how do you sell it? How do you attract people to your place of business and make them spend money? Your place of business could be an office or a store or even a post office box. Perhaps you work at home. Since zoning laws in many residential areas prohibit you from conducting business out of your house—especially if your street might turn into a parking lot—working out of the home presents its own problems, a topic for another book. But the rest of us want customers to come to us; in most cases this requires that they drive (or walk) somewhere. Different people have different shopping habits. Some will walk for blocks and shop dozens of stores until they find the right price. Some people "have to park out front." Others will "buy from a good salesperson" no matter the price. There are so-called "impulse buyers." In fact, impulse buyers have a per-ceived or real need to satisfy. The fact that they do one-stop shopping doesn't mean they have given the purchase no thought. They know what they want when they see it. Still other people will look around, wait a day or two, and return to the place that offered the best price or the best service.

MOTIVATIONS TO BUY

Some people are motivated by brand loyalty. Why are you a Republican or Democrat? Probably because your parents were; it's the same reason you buy Buicks or Fords; Ivory soap or Dial. There are so many choices of cars, soap, toothpaste, and the like, that it helps to have a reason to narrow the field — any reason. Habit is one reason. Price is a strong motivator when there is no real difference between products. Availability sometimes makes our choices for us. Just how many restaurants serve Diet Orange Slice, or both Pepsi and Coke?

Proximity often determines where people shop for food and clothing. The nearest grocery store and the neighborhood shopping mall require the least amount of mental and physical effort, especially since frequenting the same places eventually helps us save time. Don't you have your local grocery store memorized so that you can go directly to most of the items you habitually buy? Wouldn't traveling to a different store with a different layout prove confusing and time consuming? Of course.

If you plan to start a retail business, locating your shop near the people whom you hope to attract only makes sense. If you will sell cars, you need more space. People who aren't brand loyal car shoppers want to look at everything. Once they have determined their "needs" — a car, a truck, a van — they will find out who is selling the best vehicle at the best price. These people will travel from dealer to dealer; so it makes sense to put your dealership close to others.

Service businesses, like photocopy and printing shops, also benefit from proximity to customers. It makes more sense to have a legal brief copied at the shop in the lobby of your law firm's high rise than to walk or drive a block to a competitor, since prices and quality are fairly uniform in the industry.

LOCATION

So the first thing you can do to give your business a chance for success is *choose a good location.* Examine what you will sell and how much competition you'll have. Then consider the shopping habits of your potential customers (like those described above). Cheap rent in an invisible location may enable you to launch your business, but it won't keep it going unless your product or service is so special that it creates both demand and a willingness in people to go out of their way to get it. Charlie's roll-top desks are like that. He doesn't need much walk-in business; his production capacity is limited. The exposure his product gets at trade shows creates continuous demand.

PRICE SHOPPERS AND SERVICE SHOPPERS

People are "price shoppers" or "service shoppers." Quality factors into either decision-making process.

The price shopper has decided what item to buy and is going to "look for the best deal." The lowest price may or may not be the best deal. You can purchase a ten-speed bike for $100, but you'll have to assemble it, and if you put a part on wrong and break something, the company you purchased it from offers no warranty. All bicycle pedals screw on forward. Screwing a part on is typically taken for granted. It's the one part of the instructions that people fail to read. It usually costs them a new pedal. For those who fancy themselves, or who really are, mechanically inclined, a bike in a box is a bargain. For others, it could be a real danger. Ten speeds rely on wire to hold to hold the tension of the brake and derailleur (gear changer). When a newly assembled bike is put together by a bike shop, these wires are tightened. The home mechanic may forget to do this. A month later, or sooner, the wires need retightening, and again about once a year.

So what is it worth to you to make certain your brakes work? $150? If the shop offers periodic adjustments, $200. In that case the "best deal" for the lowest price is the price of the bike and the service. Cars are more complex. And while anyone can, in fact, adjust bike brakes with a wrench and a pair of pliers, cars require more knowledge and larger, more expensive tools. When they install the monorail in our town, I'll save automobile travel for vacations. Meanwhile, I'll gladly pay more than sticker price to get the car serviced and maintained by the dealer under an extended warranty. This sort of offer is not always available. But the one time it was, that dealer got my business. Again, the lowest price is relative to what you expect to own for your money. Even groceries, a commodity often advertised by relative pricing, reflect this fact. In the summer, a 25 cents a pound head of lettuce will do if I plan to use it that evening; but if I'm stocking the refrigerator for the week, I'd look for a head that will last longer, and I'll expect to pay more.

The irony of pricing is how hard so many businesses work to be the "low price leader." Being the cheapest does not mean people will flock to your door. A lot of companies behave that way. But their rivals typically match their low prices during special sales, so "lowest" becomes relative to price, quality, and service.

Price your products realistically. Calculate (on paper) your cost of doing business. Project your overhead and cost of production, salaries, supplies, etc. Add to that what you would like to earn in salary (be conservative in the first two years). Measure your prices against the competition's — not to match their prices but to find out what they are really selling at their prices. The competitor who sells bikes in a box is going to be the "cheapest." Let that company have that market. In small business, a better strategy is to charge enough to offer quality and service along with your product. Carry a higher quality bike, for example, and offer to adjust the brakes for free for a year.

Pricing Problems

Perhaps you are thinking as you read this, if you can sell a *lot* of "the cheapest" bikes, you can make more money and attract more customers. Let me clarify. What enables one company to be "the cheapest" is its ability to buy large quantities of a single product. This presents two problems for the small business owner. First, a large quantity requires a large outlay of capital for a single item. If you are just starting, you probably should not risk that much capital on a single product (unless it is your only product — like the pet rock). What if it does not sell? Is your cash reserve large enough to sell all those bikes at cost, or less, and purchase a new inventory, which in all likelihood will cost you more? If you sell seasonal items, like women's clothing, you cannot afford that kind of mistake. It takes three to six months for an order of clothing to arrive. You have to shop for each season that far in advance. If you get stuck with a large inventory of a single style, you not only won't make money, you won't be able to reorder soon enough to recover.

Leave the price cutting wars to the big chains (Sears, K-Mart, JC Penney), the discount stores, and manufacturers' wholesale outlets. The large retailers buy merchandise for stores around the country. When they purchase a thousand of a single item, each store in the chain receives a small fraction of the order. The risk is spread out — since each store carries a wide variety, a single unpopular (unsellable) item won't cause a catastrophe.

Storage

The second problem a small retailer faces is storage. Where are you going to put it all? You should not waste rent money on excess storage space. Your inventory should always be on display for the customer to see and select from. Spend your rent on showroom space, not storage. Pewter by Ricker II uses the cabinets underneath the display shelves to store most of its inventory. When the single item on the shelf is sold, the manager replaces it immediately and easily. Furthermore, if a customer wants to compare the detailing on two figurines of the same design, the salesperson can pull a second out from under the shelf, without leaving the customer's presence. The back room is used for layaways. When a customer who has paid a deposit on a pewter sculpture watches the salesperson go into the back room to get his or her "layaway," it gives the impression that the customer's purchase was, in fact, put aside just for that customer. On the other hand, when a salesperson leaves the floor to find something in the back room, it gives a person who is "just looking" an excuse to leave the store. Many people won't ask whether you have more of an item if they can't see it on display. So if you forget to pull something out of the back room and put it on the shelf or rack, you could lose business.

Shoe stores are a notable exception. Since we were little children, we've been trained to sit down, take off our shoes, and have a salesperson find our size. Shoe stores need only one pair (even one shoe) on display. Then the salesperson runs in and out of the back room to bring different styles, colors, and sizes to his or her customer. Payless Shoe Source changed this system with mass merchandising. Their merchandise is minimum quality, and each store's entire inventory is on display in the showroom. Once a salesperson has explained the stores' system — where you can find your size — you are on your own while you try on shoes. Help is available if you need it, but you have to ask. Quantity buying for a large number of stores has enabled Payless to capture a significant share of the low price market.

SHOULD YOU BUY IN QUANTITY?

If you have enough start-up capital to afford quantity buying, a large enough store to display your merchandise, and a large enough advertising budget to let a television/newspaper audience know you exist, do it. You'll need all three: quantity, space, and exposure — lots of it. McDonald's sells billions of hamburgers because millions of people have heard the name over and over. Furthermore, you can find a McDonald's in almost every town and city all over the country, even the world.

The small retailer or service company should offer more for the price he or she has to charge. Shoe stores that hire salespeople to help customers sell better goods. The electronics company that sells a higher priced camera will help you learn to use it, and will offer a limited warranty. The bike store will assemble your purchase and adjust it for a reasonable period of time (flat tires not included).

SELL QUALITY AND SERVICE

This is the type of business the beginner with limited capital wants to be in. You have a better chance of staying in business over a longer period of time if you sell quality and service, rather than the cheapest price. Price must be a factor of your costs plus a markup to cover overhead, expenses, and your income.

Every business owner I have interviewed made the same comment regarding his or her success: "I owe it all to my employees." The employees (and you, if you deal directly with customers) control how much quality and service your company offers customers. You might sell the finest Italian leather shoes available in your city. They will last four years with everyday wear. But what if no one tells the customer? Say the customer is in the habit of buying $20 shoes, which she expects to last "the season." Fifty dollars to her is an "outrageous" price for shoes, unless you offer more. The shoes aren't going to tell her that they last longer. A person has to say it. A salesperson not only has to say it, but must point out the construction features of the shoes so that the customer can "see it" for herself. That is how you sell quality and service, by attending to the customer's "real need" (to buy a pair of shoes) and "perceived need" (to buy a pair of shoes that will last, fit, feel comfortable, and provide good value for the money).

Judy Harris, owner of Classy Lady, estimates that 75% of her business comes from repeat customers. "I hope it's because they like the clothes and the one-on-one service," she says. Judy and her staff agree that shopping remains a popular activity, but some things have changed. They say they have observed that both Classy Lady stores have a large crowd on Saturdays' but many professional women don't have a lot of time to shop, even though "they have more money to spend than ever before." Since clothes cost more, women have turned toward "investment buying" — buying things that match previous years' purchases and that will last. Classy Lady's staff is part of Judy's success, she says, because they realize this and cater to it.

Judy avoids spending her capital on trendy fashions. She says any small business must specialize, then service customers well. "I try to hire people whose lifestyles are most like my customers'. The customers feel that. When someone comes out of a fitting room, we want them to look wonderful in the clothes, and when they go out, have people ask, 'Where did you get that?' Referrals are our best advertisement." Judy solicits input from her staff when she makes buying decisions, since they have the closest contact with the clientele.

That is what you should look for in employees — people who are as interested in the future of your company as you are. Look for people who want to help you make wise decisions about your business, like Judy's staff who keep her informed about her customers' tastes and preferences.

What can you do to find this type of person? Part of it has to do with your hiring process. People like this are born, not made. They will be interested in becoming a part of your organization the day they start with you. The extent to which they behave this way depends on you — on your ability to manage and motivate. More about managing in a future chapter.

GETTING CUSTOMERS IN THE DOOR

Before your employees work their magic, you have to attract people into your place of business. People become customers only after they have bought something. Part of your management function is to get people in the door (or orders in the mailbox). I've discussed advertising and public relations at some length. These are your starting points. Ads will build name recognition and, if designed well and targeted to the right audience, will attract the number of prospects you need to get started. Everyone who responds to an ad favorably will encourage a friend to try your store. An ad will simply get a warm body with a real or perceived need in your door. Ads will also attract "browsers" — people whose needs are still in the subconscious. How you keep people in your store depends on a combination of your sales techniques, your inventory, your pricing (relative to quality and service), and your display.

Display

Display is important. How you arrange products in your place of business will have an effect on your success. If your product is a physical object, attractive display is a matter of arranging items so that the customer is filled with a sense of abundance, cleanliness, and completeness: abundance of choices, clean displays and products, and a complete selection of sizes and styles. Of course, it is not possible to carry every size or style imaginable. It just has to look that way. A customer needs to feel that shopping in your place of business provides him or her with all the choice he or she wants. Too much choice can be confusing. If one store carried every Lladro piece in the collection, the buyer would be hard pressed to "pick a favorite." One store needs to carry a good selection — something for each incremental price range. Then the store needs to add a few new pieces on a regular basis so the serious collector will have a reason to return.

Display can do a lot to accomplish all of the above. The gift shop with one long, low display case packed with items of about the same price and size causes confusion. A potential customer has too much to look at, too many decisions to make. The gift shop that uses a vertical, glass-shelved display case, with a dozen items in a spacious array, gives the customer a clear view of each item, and narrows the choices. How much is enough? It depends on your business.

Even how your store is arranged can make a difference as to whether or not people will enter. A deep store with a narrow glass front has an advantage over a store with a wide, open, glass front, or one with no visibility from the street or mall corridor. A sufficient sampling of your merchandise should be visible to passersby to entice some to walk into the store. If everything you stock is visible from the window, why should anyone walk in? Your customers will come in, but will people who are "just browsing," who want to look around but not buy today? Unlikely. You want to entice both groups.

Think about your favorite bookstore. People browse through bookstores. I will visit a bookstore five or ten times for every purchase I make. Book lovers like to visit bookstores regularly, to plan their next book while they finish one. Bookstores place a selection of books in the window or entryway to draw people in. Then rows of bookshelves, that you cannot possibly see over, force you to wander the aisles. Too little visibility can entice shoplifting. So make certain that your staff can see the browsers, even if they can't see all the merchandise, from anyplace in the store.

Details count. Dust, missing limbs on mannequins, and fingerprints on counters take away from the impression you are trying to create. Display is an art. Large department stores hire full-time display personnel. While you might be talented or have an employee who is, don't cut corners. Professional freelance display artist Sue Molitoris says, "It's aggravating to see a hand backwards, a dirty floor, a burned out light, or an undressed mannequin. The average customer may not see it, but it makes an impression. Lights are important. They need to be used, not just pointed toward the floor." Sue organizes her displays around what stores have in stock. "If they have only one of something, someone will want it and we'll have to take the window apart ten minutes later." She says one client had twenty plaid dresses that were not selling, so she put a vest and matching accessories on the dress in the display windows, and the store sold out. Brent Erkelens, art and advertising director at O.C. Tanner Jewelers, says, "I think windows are better advertising than advertising. They get a lot of attention. And to see them, you have to go by the store and see where it is."

Your display should catch attention. Make people stop, literally, to look at your displays and put themselves in the scene or the item on display in their own scene (home, recreation, work). Should you hire a professional? My suggestion is, if you don't have a lot of natural artistic ability and a little on-the-job training, a professional will give you the edge. Like advertising, it is possibly one expenditure of capital that will give you an edge over the competition, and it should pay for itself.

Banners and Posters

Banners and posters are two other visual items used to attract attention. Most shoppers these days want prices clearly marked, People have less time to shop and therefore, less time to spend trying to figure out prices. It's like trying to remember a restaurant's list of daily specials. You might catch one or two, but you'll have to ask the waiter to repeat the rest and this can get annoying. Use price tags. Banners on everything make things look like sale items when they are not. Unless you live in New York, where parking is horrible so people do less comparison shopping, people do comparison shop. They compare not only you and your competitors, but your prices and inventory from one day to the next. If your "regular price" is made to look like a "sale price" because of flashy signs, you'll lose credibility. Your customers will have less reason to respond to any "real" sale you advertise in the paper or on television/radio. If everything is always on sale, then nothing ever really is. Most people spend time pondering their perceived needs and they *wait* for the right item at the right price. Keep yourself in the competition with honesty.

SALES, PROMOTIONS, DISCOUNTS

How can you expect to fool people who come into your store once a week/ month by hanging posters that make the same price look like a special deal? You can't. A "special promotion" should be just that — special, meaning unique: lower prices for a limited period of time. Salt Lake's Downtown Retail Merchants Association (DRMA) sponsors a semi-annual sidewalk sale, sometimes in conjunction with the two downtown malls. Merchants on Main Street and those in the malls push a lot of inventory onto the sidewalk or into the corridors. The event is heavily promoted. Having been employed in the downtown area for eleven years and gone to almost every such sale, I noticed that very few of the merchants offer anything on sale at the sidewalk sales that wasn't on sale inside the store the previous day and won't be on sale in the store the following week. Again, I had the advantage of working downtown. The suburbanite who travels to town twice a year — for the sidewalk sales — may not be aware of this. So it does attract some business.

However, there is one gift store on Main Street, Shapiro's, that is a notable exception. Their "sale" really is one — limited in time and large in quantity. Operated by the founder's son, who employs his own two sons, Shapiro's has built an image of excellence for luggage and gifts. I shop there not only during their sidewalk sales, but anytime I want a tasteful gift. I appreciate their honesty and the occasional good deal. I feel good about patronizing an honest business person.

While I personally don't spend a moment of my time fighting the crowd to look at stuff I know to be on permanent sale, these events are popular in Salt Lake. It gives the merchants an opportunity to move old or dated merchandise, gain exposure for their product line, and it creates a media event for the downtown area. Department stores have a chance to put a sampling of all their wares — usually spread over four floors or more — on view. It's a way to show people who have never ventured into the housewares department what the store carries. For the small merchant with limited inventory, most sidewalk sales are an excuse to get rid of junk. Most people recognize junk when they see it. But even junk — unsold merchandise — will find a buyer if the price is right, and the merchant has just that much less cash tied up in something that will never sell.

A sidewalk sale is another type of display. For people who have never ventured into your store, it gives them a good look at what you carry if you put your usual merchandise on display, rather than those things you want to get rid of and don't intend to carry anymore. Keep this in mind if you have the opportunity to participate in this type of event.

The "Sale" has become a standard way of doing business for many large department stores. There's the everyday low price sale, the every weekend sale, and the "real" sale. A specialist in the everyday sale, Mr. Mac (Mac Christiansen), a Utah clothing retailer, trains salespeople to attach themselves to a client as soon as one walks in the door. If you express interest, or even disinterest, the salesperson will go "talk with Mac," return, and tell you the "real price," which is predictably half of the marked price, if the price is marked, or half the original price the salesperson told you. People who shop regularly, like myself, have come to understand how the game is played. I find one of my two regular salesmen, so as not to be pestered by the others, and have him help me. They keep records of their customers' purchases, so they can offer me real assistance finding the right sizes, and a suit or shirt that will match the rest of Budd's wardrobe. Except for the everyday-saleness of the system, they offer the same service as the people at Classy Lady. But it can be a little overwhelming for the uninitiated; and I know people who won't enter the store because, they say, "the salespeople are so pushy." Well, in his favor, Mac has operated a successful business for years. He has relocated his downtown Mr. Mac store four times in the last decade, too. He stocks a huge selection of men's clothing, and more recently women's, and for the quality of clothing he offers, no one can touch his prices. Once you find one salesperson to deal with, it is a pleasant system.

Could a newcomer copy it? Mac buys for his stores around the state. Each store has a large selection, so a salesperson's help to narrow the choices is legitimate. And since his salespeople tend to stay with him for years, a customer can deal with a single individual, who has kept records, over a long period of time. Since Mac's son Scott works there, I would venture to guess there will be at least one salesperson I will deal with for as long as the company remains in business. The company really sells service. They even offer lifetime free tailoring on any of their merchandise, even if you lose fifty pounds, as one acquaintance of mine did.

Inkley's, as do many electronics stores, always lists the "manufacturer's suggested retail price" on the bar coded label. That price is crossed out and Inkley's price is listed below it. This is another way to make a customer feel well treated. Is it real? No. Inkley's pricing, like everyone else's, regardless of the product or service for sale, is determined by its inventory costs, overhead, percent return on investment (profit margin), etc. The manufacturer's suggested retail price is, essentially, an imaginary number.

If your price is never really our price, you can expect customers to wait for your *best* price. Once you set the precedent of having regular sales, you can expect the majority of people who are in the market for what you sell (have a perceived need) to wait for your special deal. Is this a good way to run a business? If all of your competitors operate that way, you may have to, to compete. Run your sales when the competition runs theirs and invite those sale-shoppers to compare. But don't sell things for less than they cost you. A lot of companies behave this way to match the competition's prices. Let your competitors sell for less than cost. Soon enough, they will not be competing.

Cost Items and Profit Items

If you do sell something for cost to match the competition, try to pair it with an item that will make you money: a camera (cost) and a camera bag (profit), lettuce (cost) and a basket full of other groceries (profit), a necktie (cost) and a shirt to match (profit). The concept of selling lettuce at cost and a basketful of groceries is commonly accepted by grocers and their customers. Once someone comes into your store for the lettuce, he or she is likely to pick up other needed items. The other examples are less obvious. The trick of selling one item at cost (or on sale) with another at a profit is training your salespeople (yourself, too) to service customers. It is called *suggestion selling*, and volumes have been written about it. Simplified, it means when someone comes to your store in response to the advertised special, the salesperson or clerk has to (not should, has to) say, "Now such and such would go nicely with that" or "Would you like a such and such to put that in?" A talented, trained salesperson will make the two items seem essential, inseparable, and important to the customer. And once presented, the idea will seem *obvious* to the client — something he or she would have thought of, given the time. A camera needs a bag; a shirt needs a tie; even lettuce needs salad dressing.

Customer Service

This is customer service. Whether you sell on-sale or as-marked, customer service matters more than anything else if you want to build a clientele of repeat customers. This does not include "bargain hunters" or the poor. We are talking about people who have enough money to cater to their perceived needs, as well as, or rather than, their real needs. Those who need clothes because the old ones are worn out past repair will price shop. They will put up with rude salespeople if the price is cheap. But if you are trying to get a share of America's discretionary income, set your sights higher.

If you are starting a small business on little capital, how can you hope to compete with the discounts of low-price retailers? They buy from Hong Kong and Korea in huge quantities for their chain of stores. Forget it. As a small business you should set your sights on middle to upper income shoppers. These people want service. They want quality. They will recognize quality if they get service. Your goal should be to sell everything in your store for "list price."

The weekend sale is a variation of the all-the-time sale. The bargain hunters wait for the weekends. The people who hate crowds shop weekdays and pay more. It's a decent way to get people in the store during an otherwise slow time. But advertising costs are very high. A small retailer or service business would be hard pressed to afford the television time.

The "real sale" is unpredictable, or so seldom as to be hard to remember. Nordstrom has real sales, as does Shapiro's gifts. Once or twice a year, they clear their inventory. The price reductions are dramatic, the time period limited. Both sell leftover or seasonal merchandise to people who could not otherwise afford to shop there. But the sale prices are still high enough to dissuade the "bargain hunter" or the poor. Nordstrom attracts the upwardly mobile who need a nice wardrobe and who will continue to shop there during and after their climb up the ladder (or their spouse's). The "real sale" builds customer loyalty.

Visibility

There are other, less obvious ways to "sell" your business. Make your company name visible. When CSB changed its name to Key Bank, management gave gold key lapel pins to all the employees. As these people interact with the public, both in the bank or in a restaurant at lunch, their pins advertise the company. It plants name recognition in people's minds. A lapel pin gives strangers something to talk about. ("Oh, what a cute pin. Is that Key Bank?") Uniforms are another way to create recognition. Most fast food restaurants issue uniforms for this reason (and because polyester is easier to clean daily than street clothing). Hats, name badges, a t-shirt printed with the company's logo—all are ways to tell people who enter your store where they are and who they are dealing with.

People learn to recognize and equate certain colors with certain products. Watch yourself the next time you shop for staples at the grocery store. Don't you reach for the package before you read the name? That's because you recognized the colors and design and didn't have to read the name. That same "packaging" can work for you in your retail or service business. You probably won't want to ask your bookkeeper to wear a uniform or a name tag, but do invest in a desktop nameplate for your entire office staff. It is more comfortable for a repeat customer to read someone's name and then greet that person by name with a prompt, than to start a conversation with, "Now what is your name?" Make people feel at ease. Make them shop by the packaging. Again, the more effort you take out of the process, the more people will habitually patronize your place of business.

Guy, The Ringmaker, wears a green jeweler's apron with his logo imprinted on the front. Every time he visits a supplier or goes to the bank, people can see where he works. He is a walking billboard. Find ways for you and your employees to become walking billboards, too. Even your automobile should have a painted or magnetic sign on the side that displays the name of your business. Of course, you must keep your car in good repair — fix dents and scratches immediately. Anything you can do to get your name seen or heard by the public is part of selling.

GETTING REPEAT BUSINESS

Once you get prospects into your place of business, meet or surpass their expectations. Every business owner who knows that success is based on repeat business will tell you his customers return because of the service he and his employees give. When I owned Midnight Oil Typesetting, I counted on about a dozen people, who represented small businesses, non-profit organizations and large corporations, to bring me their monthly ad, monthly newsletter, annual price list changes, and menu changes to typeset. The same people came back again and again. Without them, I would have gone broke. One of my former customers owned a business at one time that did go broke when three of his regular clients declared bankruptcy within a month of one another.

You should never narrow your customer base too much. Expect some of your regulars to stop shopping at your business. Some stop because of financial problems, others will have moved out of the area. But every customer you treat well, who comes back again, is gold.

Customers whom you treat well should treat you well too. Beware the ones who are never satisfied, who are always looking for what's broken before they even pay for it. The people you can never please are not worth your time and effort because they are either looking for a reason not to pay you, or they are going to take up so much of your time and mental energy making them happy that you will lose a dozen other customers who would require only your normal time and effort to please. People who complain about problems that you know have no basis in fact are often out to get something for nothing. They want a special discount on a camera, a free ad in your magazine, and a *lot* of your time. Don't give anything away without a reason. Be polite. Remember, they have friends, too, and word-of-mouth can work both ways. But assert yourself and tell these people that things that are not broken cannot be fixed. Follow up by saying, "How can I really help you?" In retail, your loss will be time. In service or other businesses that rely on in-house credit, the chronic complainer will cost you time and money. However, if you make the "sale" correctly, you can avoid a lot of combat.

Dealing with Complaints

You have to learn to distinguish the chronic complainers from those who complain because they have a misunderstanding. Sometimes a gap in the sales process has created that misunderstanding. Remember, making a "sale" must include establishing worth, value, and agreement to exchange product for dollars. The most frequent complaint we heard at Edna's publishing company was that the client had gotten no calls the week after the ad appeared in our magazine. The food places, selling 50 cent ice cream cones for 25 cents seldom had that problem. The high-end retailers and professionals—jewelers, fur dealers, lawyers, and doctors—complained without fail. People don't call the doctor unless they need to. Few people buy furs and jewelry the moment they see an ad. Again, people react to advertising when they already have a perceived need. They wait for the right time to satisfy that need. Wanting something, having the time to shop for it, and having the money (now or over time) to pay for it are all factors in the buying process.

I often wondered why salespeople never explained that to their clients. Nevertheless, those who protested the most were typically the ones who did not pay their bills. They never agreed that advertising had value, so they looked for "reasons" not to pay. Not having the phone ring off the hook was a "reason." To Edna, it was an "excuse." An incomplete sales process had created the situation, nevertheless.

SHOULD YOU NOT SELL TO SOME PEOPLE?

Part of successful selling is knowing whom not to sell to. Don't sell to people who have no money. Some people will say they don't have money just so a salesperson either leaves them alone or works harder to find out what to do to make the sale. If the person really has no money, you'll find out when you're ready to close the sale ("How would you like to pay for that today?") and are told no ("I don't have any money now") just before the person leaves the store. When you sell on contract and credit, you have to be even more careful. You have to determine both willingness and ability to pay.

Potential debtors who have no money will actually tell you so. An ad insertion contract, for example, presumes creditworthiness. Listen to the things people tell you as though they were filling out a credit application. "I'm just starting in business, and I don't really have a budget for advertising," or "I just got out of Chapter 11 and we're trying to recover," should tell you that this client is not a good credit risk. These people might be future customers. The future might be now if, "I don't have the money," is an excuse, not a real reason. A good salesperson can move such an "objection" into a sale. But if that person really doesn't want to or cannot afford to buy and feels pressured into signing a contract to pay later, you'll spend an inordinate amount of time trying to collect.

Nevertheless, many merchants knock themselves out to make it possible for people who can't pay for something to have it anyway. Some methods are legitimate, others are courting bad debt. Putting something on layaway is the only legitimate way for a start-up company to turn a hopeful into a buyer. Even so, the salesperson must make it clear that a layaway deposit is forfeit if the customer changes his or her mind. The fact remains that the hopeful does not gain possession of the merchandise until it is paid for in full, and there is a limited time period that you are obliged to have that item removed from your inventory for sale.

Other systems, like the "Payment Plan" or "We'll hold your check until Friday," are foolish if you part with product or service first and you don't have enough working capital to also be in the finance business. You have just given your hopeful the perfect excuse never to pay you: "Well, I didn't have the money and you pressured me into placing an ad," or, "I thought I was going to get paid by one of my customers on Friday so I could pay you, but I didn't get paid." I heard these both a lot at my last job. And when the bankruptcy notices arrived in the mail, my employer's chances of collecting at all dropped to zero. Yet I watched her give credit to people who were obviously not credit-worthy, who told her so, and who did not even put a deposit on the order to cover expenses. If it happens to you, you will spend months, years even, on the telephone (or in court) trying to collect. All that time should be spent servicing clients who do business with the company regularly and pay their bills, as well as soliciting new business. It's sad that the bad debts command more attention than the loyal customers when you extend credit.

EFFECTIVE SELLING

Everything depends on how effectively you sell. Remember, "the sale," like any legal contract, is based on understanding and agreement. A signature is not a sale. Don't sell to people who do not want to buy from you and tell you so both by their words and by their unwillingness to give you any money (payment in full or a deposit). Move on to the next name on your callback list or the next person on the sales floor. It takes an astute salesperson to tell when a "browser" has become a "potential buyer." Make browsing comfortable (except for shoplifters), but don't spend too much time forcing browsers into making credit purchases, unless the credit and the risk belong to a credit card company or bank. Wait until a browser's mental state is that of a potential buyer — someone with a real or perceived need — then use those sales techniques to close the sale and collect your money.

DON'T OVEREXTEND CREDIT

Don't sell to people who stop paying you. If you do extend credit to a regular customer and he or she doesn't pay the bill for a month or two, tell the client you will not sell anything else to him or her until you are paid in full. Also request that any future purchases be paid for with cash, in full.

A lot of business owners don't do this because they are afraid they'll lose a customer, or worse, a friend. You will lose neither. People who don't pay you are not customers. People who owe you a great deal of money will go out of their way to stop doing business with you. They may feel guilty, they certainly don't want to receive daily phone call reminders about how much money they owe you, and they don't want to get in any deeper, unless they are thieves. You can avoid both thieves and the honest business people who simply spent more than they could afford and now can't or won't pay your bill, by saying "no" when the accumulated debt is two months old. Why not three or four? Because you have a chance of collecting on a month or two of back debt.

The last year I owned my business, two of my best customers (and favorite people) went bankrupt. Both paid my bill before they did. One left the state, the other took Chapter 11 and eventually sold out (John Felt's Heritage Keepsake). But before that happened, I called on them often to find out if I could do any more work for them. I had extended both credit. (I never let a bill get more than thirty days old before I personally went to collect and never did more work until the old bill was paid.) I would drop by periodically and solicit business. The business never came my way. I felt bad and started to wonder what I was doing wrong — what I was doing to make them unhappy. I wondered if I had lost these two customers to some other type-setter. I tried to figure out why they didn't use my services any longer.

I found out why after they both went out of business. It was because they thought enough of me and how I ran my business that they did not want me to be a victim of their circumstances. Long before a business goes bankrupt, the owner will know that it is a likely possibility. Your "good customers" will not want you to be one of the losers if the worst should happen. They won't tell you the real problem. They'll just avoid you and make excuses for not giving you more business. Be friendly, don't beg, and avoid deals too good to refuse. You can put yourself on the creditors' list if you try hard enough. Don't. When people can't pay, or stop paying, work a little harder to find a new paying customer. Spend very little time on the non-paying customers; preferably no time at all. Just a polite, "Hello," when you pass them on the street or see them in small claims court.

12

MANAGEMENT

There are lots of books and theories about management. Most deal with corporations. Managing people who work for your small business is quite a different art. From what I have observed, the motivators are rearranged.

Perhaps this is because corporations tend to hire highly qualified people, continue to train them throughout their careers, and pay them what they "are worth." Small businesses tend to hire the range from highly qualified people to totally unskilled people; training lasts one week, if at all, and pay is proportional to "what the business can afford." The dynamics are different.

Everyone expects to earn more over time, as they increase their skills and efficiency on the job. Large public corporations (not small companies that have incorporated) have more capital. They can afford to give cost of living and merit raises regularly. Small start-up companies operate on a survival budget. No matter how deserving an employee, the money may not be available to give a raise.

THE CORPORATE PICTURE

Traditionally, large corporations hired employees with the expectation of getting thirty years of work from their people. This attitude is less prevalent today, with mergers and layoffs and two-income couples who follow different career paths. The traditional "wife" who followed her husband from city to city in pursuit of his climb up the ladder is harder to find these days; sometimes the husband chooses that role.

Small businesses may want to hire lifetime employees. But that is unrealistic. The factors that influenced the traditional thirty-year employee to stay were: salary, benefits, pension plans, and power. Start-ups will spend one to five years struggling to pay bills and minimal salaries, while putting a little cash aside for expansion or change. There just isn't any money for pension plans. Benefits tend to include employee discounts on what the company sells, co-payments on health and dental insurance, and the annual company picnic or Christmas party. This doesn't even come close to the expense accounts and club memberships that a corporate executive can expect to receive as a matter of course. As one's salary gets higher, so do taxes. At some point, a raise will lower one's net income; so benefits (which are not taxable to the employee, and these rules have changed lately) are the tie that binds.

I have had my boss supply a pizza on nights I've worked until 10:00 p.m. But I know I could have afforded that pizza; furthermore, the only time I ate pizza was on nights I worked late. In other words, receiving something that I would not buy for myself, if I had the money to do it doesn't count as a benefit — not when I measure job satisfaction and motivation to stay. Receiving benefits that I would spend my money on anyway does count. Complimentary ballet tickets are money in my pocket.

Managing employees at a small firm requires a different type of effort than doing the same for a corporation. Corporate employees are paid highly not only for their job abilities but for their social skills. Part of the game is to get along with a large number of people in the office and socially outside of work. Small companies require that their employees co-exist in the office place. If they socialize outside the office, it is usually based on genuine friendship and mutual interests. Since there is seldom, if ever, a ladder to climb, there is no need or call for ladder-climbing behavior patterns. Mentorism is irrelevant when the only job higher than yours is the owner's.

Since getting along is a byproduct of genuine attraction on the part of co-workers in a small business, it is harder to find people who will get along. They don't have to work to "get ahead" just to "stay put." In a small company, people really do get along from the start, or they never will. Corporate employees have to deal with hundreds of personalities. It is unlikely that so many people will have enough in common to get along well all the time. They simply have to "put up with each other."

BUILDING A TEAM

The first thing you should try to accomplish as the owner of a new small business is building a "team." You have to hire people not only on the basis of their skills and how well you (the owner) like them, but also how well your entire staff gets along. In a small company, people who get along well will work longer and harder for you.

One way to build this type of staff is to include your current employees in any decision to hire a new person. Have everyone sit in on your second interview with applicants. Ask what they think. First impressions are often misleading. You and your staff may decide at a future date that you made a mistake about whom you accepted, and a few good prospects who were too shy to make a good first impression may be lost to you. But people who like each other are more likely to put in those late night hours to help one another.

Did you think they worked long and hard to help you … the boss? To some degree this is true. But there is an unwritten rule that keeps bosses and employees separated outside of the office, which is as it should be. How can you be objective and supervise, hire or fire, if an employee follows you home for poker games or family reunions? Don't do it, even if you feel a friendship building. Keep some distance so you can still manage. Lunches outside the office can work, if you talk business.

THE WORK ENVIRONMENT

When the going gets tough and the hours get long, people put in extra time and effort to help their friends — their co-workers. Since the money for regular raises simply will not exist in the early years, your employees are going to be further motivated to remain in your employ if they have a great deal of control over their work environment. The biggest factor is whom they work with. Light, music or silence, work systems, etc., are the other things that your employees want to control. Do you insist that employees straighten their desks at the end of the day? If so, you are taking away some of the control that your people seek. The fact is, while bosses care about neat desks, customers seldom do. If an artist's or salesperson's desk is cluttered during the workday, and that person is working at his or her desk, clutter represents how they get work done. To insist they do it differently may slow them down, or sabotage a "system." Within reasonable limits, allow your staff control over their environment.

How about music versus silence? Everyone has an opinion. I cannot work with background music, and as a business owner I would not impose my taste in entertainment (talk radio) on my customers. I consider silence the only professional option. I don't know how people concentrate on work and tune out music. Some say they do, but I have watched a co-worker's attention to detail deteriorate while she stayed plugged into the stereo with a headset. Her errors started to cost the company a great deal of money, and her supervisor told her to stop. I would not risk it. You have to decide for your own workplace. Retailers who sell records or audio-visual equipment have televisions and record players turned on all the time. Their employees must consider that type of work environment satisfactory, or they would not be there. But in a professional office or service store, the work being done and the amount of concentration required should dictate the degree of silence.

Consider one other thing: silence is never complete. Every office has noise generated by office equipment and heating/air conditioning systems. These sounds cause distraction. Total silence can be a problem too. People need little breaks from work. And while music may give people an excuse not to think about or do work, a more productive way exists for people to take mental breaks — talk. People will talk to one another if the only other sound in the room is silence. The way that relationships are built — the way people communicate their demands and needs to one another — is by talking. Yes, you can create a paper flow of office memos to keep your staff informed. But talk is much better. That personal touch by you and between your employees will build a better team.

For example, I spent a summer working as a volunteer at a local pioneer history park. Most of the volunteers were unpaid. The only sounds we heard from the log cabins and adobe homes were made by wind blowing through the poplars and a howling monkey from the zoo across the street (which sounded like a bird). Talking to the other volunteers came very naturally and easily. We had common ground to discuss — the park and the visitors — and when there were no visitors, we had little else to do except quilt, tat, weave, and talk.

The majority of the volunteers returned the following summer. They had built the kind of working relationship with one another that every small business owner should aspire to. The curator of the park and the education coordinator had both taken other jobs (dissatisfied with politics and budget cuts), but it mattered not. Those volunteers worked for one another and for a "common cause" — the success of the park. That is what you, as a manager, should try to build in your company — a staff that will work for one another and for a common cause: the success of your business, which they have been made to feel a part of.

LETTING EMPLOYEES MOVE ON

Having said all that, the next thing you as an owner should expect is for people to leave your employ, especially if you are in the building years. Again, your best employees will gravitate toward money. If your company does not or cannot grow as fast as your employees' personal financial expectations, they will move on. There is nothing you can do. You can only pay what you can afford. So be prepared for the inevitable. Try not to make anyone feel mad or guilty. A former employee should continue to be your customer, even without the discount. In the best case, your business will grow rapidly and you can raise salaries to match ability, dedication, and the personal investment your best employees (and you) have (already) made. But, if not, simply write them a good recommendation and do what you can to help them find that next, higher paying job.

YOU MUST BE ABLE TO DO IT YOURSELF

Don't become too dependent on any one employee. This is easy to do. A business owner has so much to do to start a business, it is hard to keep track of it all, much less know how everything is done. As a small business owner you need to learn how *everything* is done so you can do it yourself or hire someone new and train her to do it.

Large companies tend to groom specialists. Young "management trainees" are trained by older, more experienced people. Small companies tend to hire a single specialist. When that expert gives two weeks' notice, it may not give you, the owner, enough time to find and train his or her replacement. So every time you buy a new piece of equipment, make certain you attend the classes, too. You may have to fill in for a while, or have at least enough knowledge about what needs doing to know whom to hire next. Remember, the people who started with you have one advantage — they made up their jobs.

The supplier from whom you purchased the computer trained someone to use it. That "free" training was for a single period of time, not for each new employee who comes to work for you over the years and has to use the machine. If you don't have the capital to pay for retraining each time, be the one who can do the training. At the very least, be proficient enough to recognize someone who will be able to learn more than you know on the computer, and who will be able to get the job done as well as, if not better than, the person he or she replaced. If you are a retailer, you'll probably have (or be) a sales manager to train other salespeople. But what about your bookkeeper/collection person? If you have delegated that job, which you once did yourself, and that person has set up a new system to meet the needs of your growing company (which was why you hired someone), do you understand the new system well enough to know a qualified replacement when you interview one? Is the "system" really a system according to standard accounting procedures — understandable for you, your accountant, and the IRS? It had better be, or you will spend six months playing catch-up if your bookkeeper leaves; and the IRS does not give you time to recover from incompetent help of that kind.

SALESPEOPLE

Hiring and managing competent sales help is the most difficult challenge of all for a small business owner. The one thing most salespeople are able to do well is sell themselves. That means they will convince you, during the interview, that they can sell your product or service. While they may be able to, that does not necessarily mean that they will. And just because someone has successfully sold cameras does not mean he or she can sell, for example, advertising. The first job is in a retail setting where customers come to the store, so perceived need is implied. Retail jobs are usually salaried, and it is easier to explain a physical object, like a camera, to a customer than something as intangible as advertising. Advertising is a service business, the product is intangible, pay is typically on a commission basis, and the salesperson has to make the initial contact with potential customers. He or she must be willing to spend a lot of hours calling people on the telephone to ascertain their needs, and be able to accept a lot of rejection, not to mention a lot of wear and tear on tires and shoe leather.

While salesmanship techniques can be taught, not everyone who learns them has the temperament to be a salesperson in any situation. Some people like the security of an office or a store and a salary. Others like the freedom and financial opportunity of commission selling. Since finding good people is so difficult, and training them is so time consuming, business owners tend to be incredibly reluctant to fire salespeople who don't do the job. They are even slower to fire salespeople who are good performers, but who show up late and leave early, or who don't help with the chores (paperwork, inventory, attending staff meetings) that the rest of the sales staff is expected to do. In most cases, those employees drift off on their own. They'll come in later and later, then the family portrait disappears from the desk and you get a phone call a week later that they've found another job. Inevitably, you'll find a replacement who outperforms the person you couldn't stand to see leave.

NO ONE IS IRREPLACEABLE

People are not, not, not irreplaceable. You may think so. Even they may think so. It is simply not true. Odds are, as your business grows, your skill at hiring people will improve too. Your decisions, your manager's decisions, will get better and better. Different people may have different ways of getting the same job done, which may make you uncomfortable for a time or may slow production. You have to learn to be patient and give your new employee time to learn your inventory, your prices, your production schedule, even your company's name, phone number, and address, before he or she gets up to speed. Be patient. Make certain you are familiar with everyone's job, and each staff member knows how to perform everyone else's job, so if someone leaves, you and your remaining employees can fill in for a while until the replacement catches on. Furthermore, if everyone knows a little about all the jobs, then they can help you train new people, leaving you free to sell and manage your company — very important.

When I decided to leave Edna's publishing company, people I knew told me that her company's downtown magazine would fail if I left. I told them that it would not fail because I was gone, but because the owner did too much business on trade and was running short of working capital; she had problems paying her bills on time. Edna had never made the effort to figure out what it was I did so that she, or another staff member, could fill in until a replacement was found. That, too, might herald the end of the magazine. I had trained three people to use the word processing and typesetting computer programs. A number of people in the office contributed stories to the magazine. But no one had tried to learn how I got a half dozen people to contribute stories to the magazine each month, when we did not use professional writers (except for a few public relations people) and we did not pay for articles. I have no doubt Edna could have done my job; she simply did not know what I did or how I did it. She had gone through three bookkeepers and a horrid accounting nightmare before she decided to learn the computer system. After she learned, she pronounced it "simple."

In fact, every job is "simple." We have our businesses divided into simple segments. Each job, by necessity and design, can be learned and performed by any number of people. That is how American business succeeds. We have created interdependence in the workplace, just as we have with the rest of our survival needs. It is necessary. Computers, bookkeeping, selling, even editing a magazine, have evolved into such simple systems that any company can continue to operate as employees come and go. Don't let an employee become so essential to your operation that you aren't constantly on the lookout for his or her replacement. When you rely on one person that much, he or she will know it and begin to demand more than you can afford to give — in money and management say-so. If anyone ever becomes that invaluable to the success of your business, then offer him or her a partnership, and be prepared to give up some management control. Furthermore, offer a partnership in your success, not a partnership to bail out your failure.

While money and security (pension plans and health benefits) are the most important ingredients in anyone's decision to work for you as a "career" (twenty to thirty years), there are other aspects of a "job" that will keep your employees happy and productive in the short run. Once someone has decided that money and security are priorities, you simply must meet her expectations, or expect her to look for work elsewhere. Meanwhile, try to maintain a good relationship with those people who are ready to move on, so that while they are still in your employ, you get your money's worth.

JOB SATISFACTION

Other aspects of job satisfaction include: training, experience, work environment, relationships with co-workers, control of one's time, amount of free time (days off, vacation), challenge, and participation in decisions that affect one's work life.

Priorities vary for different people. Beginners usually place heavy emphasis on training and gaining experience. As we all know, it takes experience to get hired. A few rare employers will, literally, hire someone off the street and train them. My former partner Fred Blackburn was like that. He trained anyone who expressed an interest in the quick-print business. He demanded more from his help than he did of himself, and we all preferred it when Fred did not do his own printing. He trained me. Fred was the best boss I ever had.

While I had some schooling in layout, I had never used a typesetting machine before the IBM Composer. I had used a similar machine in the military, but typestyles, fonts, kerning, and leading were foreign words to me. I spent several months reading books and memorizing terminology, trying to supplement my knowledge, because someone had given me a chance and taken the time to train me. People who are trying to break into a new field put great priority on training and experience. My former employer hired several people with limited computer experience and paid them very little while we trained them on the typesetting system and in magazine production.

Money

One's money goals build over time. Every profession requires skill building. Beginning writers often accept no pay just to see their name in print and build a portfolio. The employer who offers on-the-job training can expect to pay less than those who want all new employees to know how to use the company's specific equipment (like a particular computer program) the day they start.

Environment

Work environment can have a major impact on an employee's willingness to stay with your company. It also affects productivity. Music or silence, smoking or non-smoking, window light or fluorescent lighting do matter. They matter a lot. Even the temperature in the room will affect people's pace and attitude — sometimes their health.

The fact is, you cannot accommodate everyone all the time in a small space. You will simply have to establish a norm and know that there are some good people out there who won't work for you under those conditions. Make certain your norms are reasonable so that an equal number of good people will work for you. Unfortunately, most high rise office buildings do not have windows that open. Some in-mall retail stores don't have windows at all. On 65 degree spring days, when the automatic air conditioning system turns on, you may have to pay a higher electric bill because your staff is plugging in space heaters under the desks or counter. Live with it, or try to make an arrangement with your landlord to pay a fixed rate for electricity (i.e., included in your rent in the lease agreement).

Scientific studies indicate human beings need natural light for their physical and psychological health. Just look at the way people behave when they live under an "inversion" (polluted, dark sky) for a month. People get depressed in the dark. Fluorescent lighting is no substitute. If your store or office has no natural window light, give your employees frequent breaks, and encourage them to go outside! Many people don't take care of themselves. They "get used to" enclosed offices. Not really. Listen to your people—who gets tired two hours before the end of every day? The ones who sat in the (dark) company lounge to read and haven't seen sunlight for eight or nine hours. When this happens, encourage them to get out for some fresh air and sunlight — send them on an errand if you must.

Time

Giving your employees control over their time is another way to them to work hard for you and stay in your employ. While retail stores have to have set break times and lunch hours, so someone will be there to mind the store at all times, offices can afford to be more flexible. You could insist that break time start at 10:00 a.m. and last exactly ten minutes. But if you allow people to take breaks when they need them, they are more likely to get up from their task long enough to get a cup of coffee, then return to their desks and get back to work. Shorter, discretionary breaks will let your people know that you trust them. It builds dedication. It also averts a lot of non-productive behavior. When breaks are set in time and duration, someone has to make sure everyone follows the rules. As a business owner, do you really want to be in your office at 10:00 a.m. and at 10:10 a.m. every day to see what your people are doing? No, you should be on the telephone or on appointments building your business. If you are not, who will be? No one wants to be given the job of spy, but someone will appoint himself or herself to the same role. Someone will watch those who come in at 10:11 a.m. and get angry. An angry person is less productive. He or she will spend a lot of mental energy thinking about those other people who got eleven-minute breaks, and thinking about when to tell the boss.

Let your people control their own time as long as someone is always in the office or store to help the customers. Time cards may be necessary if you have a lot of employees and pay on an hourly basis. But if someone is ten minutes late one day (on the time card), be patient and watch for the patterns. Does he or she leave ten minutes later at the end of the day, or take a shorter lunch break the following day? If the hours add up to the forty you are paying for, and your store opens and closes on time, ignore it. Fire the people who show up late all the time if you have a policy that everyone has to be at work for a 9:00 a.m. meeting. But if one person has responsibility for opening the doors at 9:00 a.m., and you don't expect a large crowd at that hour, allow as much flexibility as you can. It makes sense to let your people come to work when there is work for them to do! If you get started at 9:00 a.m., and find that you have letters to be typed no earlier than 9:30 a.m., does it make sense to force your secretary to sit around for thirty minutes with nothing to do (assuming the previous day's work was finished)? Why not allow him or her to arrive "no later than 9:30 a.m." Flextime will spread out the pressure on the highway system in your town for one thing, and it gives your people more control over their lives.

Again, consider the personalities of your employees. There are morning, afternoon, and night people. I don't come to life until 10:00 a.m. Molly, the original art director for Edna's publishing, is a morning person. I preferred to work late; she early. We put in our "overtime" according to our own rhythms. When I first started with the company, I punched a clock. I arrived exactly at 9:00 a.m., took a 60 minute lunch, exactly, and left promptly at 6:00 p.m. During deadline week, I often worked later. Edna did not pay overtime, but I could take time off for each overtime hour I worked. I grew to resent the rigidity of my schedule, because I often didn't have anything to do until noon, when someone turned in an article, or I had an interview appointment scheduled. I renegotiated with my employer, and was able to control my own time, which meant sometimes I'd arrive at 9:00 a.m., sometimes at 2:00 p.m. I would take a two-hour lunch or none at all. But my hours and breaks were task oriented. We had a product to produce by a deadline. My job was to get my work done so that the magazine could get to press on time. My work directly affected everyone's ability to get their work done toward the same end. Molly, Charlene, and I communicated needs, expectations, and abilities with Edna and the sales force, and worked together toward that end. During the first two years, only one issue was delivered late. Six months later, communications between sales/management and production broke down completely and three publications were each three days late.

Susie, an executive secretary, also has control of her time. She can arrive between 8:00 a.m. and 10:30 a.m. and is required to work eight hours. This means if she stays out late one night, she doesn't have to drag herself to work half asleep and spend an hour downing coffee, just to put on a show that she is there. She is ready to work when she arrives and has told me that her most productive hours are after 6:00 p.m. when she, officially, "is not there." Susie Madden is also an artist. A previous employer allowed her to arrive at 7:00 a.m. so she could go home at 4:00 p.m. to prepare for an upcoming art festival. For a month, she worked two eight-hour shifts each day — one at her full-time job, and another at home each evening to produce her silkscreen prints and stationery for the festival. She was satisfied with that job and had made friends with her co-workers, but the parent company disbanded the office. Between those two jobs, she worked at a bank. During her formal evaluation, she was reprimanded for "not walking fast enough to the photocopy machine." She quit. Shortly thereafter, the bank was "taken over." Banks get taken over when they are in serious financial trouble.

In a retail or service store, you have to have an adequate number of people on the sales floor at all times to service clients. Nevertheless, you can let those people select times to go to lunch and days off. Have your employees work it out among themselves. This way, people come and go on time to help co-workers, rather than to follow some rule set by management.

Challenge

Challenge is also important. People like to feel that they are growing and progressing in life. Some look for growth in their personal lives; some at work. Career people are highly involved with their jobs. They feed their egos on their successes. Make certain your best people have new challenges; make certain those challenges are concrete and obtainable — nothing so vague as "work harder and sell more." No, you must create new opportunities to learn — ways to gain new or polish old skills. Give your best people a sense of participation in your business decision-making process and your company's future. Ask their opinions — be sincerely interested — and follow their good advice. Sometimes, you have to live with your own decisions when they are contrary to everyone else's opinion. If so, don't ask for everyone else to love your idea or give you their approval. If you ask for opinions simply get them or discuss them. Then go away and decide what to do. Some decisions have to be yours and yours alone, for better or worse. But whatever your decision, tell your staff why you decided to do what you did. Explain your reasons and your expectations of the outcome. Let them know that what they had to say was considered.

Given enough time, everyone in your organization will "have his or her way" at some time. You'll be surprised, but when things are going well, your employees will often make the same decisions you would have, because they are basing their opinions on the same information. When things are going well, employers tend to keep their employees informed.

KEEP EMPLOYEES INFORMED

When things are going poorly, employers tend to keep secrets. That is when the boss and the staff will start to disagree on everything. You may have to live with that. But don't ignore what is going on. Your employees may or may not know "better"; they simply know "less." If you want to solicit opinions that matter, make certain your people have the facts and information they need to give you a considered opinion, or don't ask.

If you and your employees are constantly at odds, something is very wrong. How can you expect your people to work hard for you, and remain loyal, dedicated employees who think they have a long and prosperous future with your business, if they don't like the way you run the company? If you decide to change the direction of your company, your people are going to be bewildered. Some will also be frightened; some will go job hunting. If you are changing the direction of your business to meet new economic and business conditions — as well you should — keep people informed. Let them know what you know, so they will also keep you informed. Some may want to leave your company anyway. But if you keep the lines of communication open, you shouldn't be caught by surprise.

If you are in so much debt that you don't know what you are doing, and you are going to try everything you can think of to get yourself out of trouble, you should still share that information. You'll find that everyone thought so anyway. In a small business, expect that everyone will know almost everything. If you are in trouble, it is only ethical to tell your people. They may stick it out or they may leave, but you will be better off if they don't spread rumors of despair while you are trying to recover. Your best people will not only be part of your success, they can also be part of your solution, if you let them.

Participation

Large corporations attract people who are security-oriented, then they offer security. Small businesses cannot offer high salary/pension plan-type security. So, they have to provide security in another form — participation. The more your people feel part of the decision-making process and are actually involved in the management of your business as it grows, the better they will feel about the company as a place to invest time and hard work. The better they feel about the company, the more they come to believe that your business is going to be successful, long lasting, and able to provide them with a secure future.

So keep talking and keep listening to your best employees — the ones you want to keep. Let the others come and go.

13

A RETURN TO THE FAMILY FARM

Much has been written about the importance and impact of "family" upon the human psyche. Most people would agree that early childhood experience sets the course for much of our adult lives. We take the morals, values, and skills our parents gave us and build upon them. We take the trauma, disappointment, and abuse and try to recover from that. It is all in us — the people, the places, the experiences, and the self that filters and interprets all that input, for better or worse.

THE EVOLUTION OF THE WORKPLACE

A century ago, America was still a land of farms and small towns. Mom and Dad and the ten children went out to the fields each day to plant and harvest, then store food for the winter. The children knew what their parents did for a living; they participated in the same tasks, and the "value" of work was survival.

The industrial age sent fathers to the cities, mothers to the suburbs, and children to schools. Suburbanite mothers were further isolated by the fact that their husbands' jobs were in cities and states far away from their own parents. In other words, mothers were on their own when it came to child rearing. Grandparental assistance was hard to come by far away from home. Fortunately for post-war suburban mothers, the labor force of teenage babysitters was ample and cheap.

Nowadays, mothers also often work outside the home. Not only must many children spend ages six to eighteen in school, but children under age six may be in day care. The result of all this absentee parenting is that children don't know their parents. They don't understand or value the work that their parents do. And children have no sense of the value of their own work — there is no logical connection between taking the trash out and putting food on the table.

THE FAMILY BUSINESS

What does all this have to do with small business? If you are just starting, not too much. But as you progress, it takes on importance if you plan to have, or already have, a family. Small business has taken the place of the family farm. It is the one situation in our modern society that allows parents to work side by side, and the children to participate in both their parents' lives and in meaningful work.

None of the entrepreneurs I've interviewed planned it this way. But certainly that has been the way things turned out for most. If you are looking for a way to combine family with career, small business seems to be an excellent setting for child rearing.

The Hales

Robert Hale was seven when his family opened their first store, The Ink Spot, an office supply store and printing shop at the time. His brothers were five and nine and their sister, born in 1963, "was raised in the back of the store." Robert says the family works six days a week; most days start at 8:00 a.m. and end well past 9:00 p.m. when the stores close. "When the first business opened," says Robert, "we (the kids) swept floors, dusted, and delivered handbills in Layton, Kaysville, and Clearfield. I've worked full-time since I was seventeen years old." By 1970, the Hales had discontinued the printing services at The Ink Spot and added a line of Hallmark cards. After college, Robert became manager of The Ink Spot, the family's most profitable store. The family, including Robert's wife, Heather, is still very close. After all, they all have something in common to discuss, on an adult level. Even family vacations center around buying trips.

The Cavanaughs

Marie Cavanaugh did not set out to be a working mother; she fell into a professional life because of her skills both as a chocolate dipper and as a business person. And she had the help (and construction skills) of her husband George. Their business grew out of a hobby and then a church fundraising project. When the demand grew so large that they spent most of their time delivering chocolates to customers in cities up to 225 miles from their South Dakota farmhouse, they relocated to Marie's home state of Utah. They picked Bountiful as the ideal location because there were no other chocolate factories there and, says Marie, "Bountiful is beautiful. Ideal for us and our five kids."

They purchased a building from a local utility company and converted the front offices into a home and the six-truck garage into a factory. Their five employee staff grew to seventy-three by 1988. Marie carries as many photographs of her family as she does of her business. She even names her signature chocolates after her grandchildren, like "Mindy Mints." "I was a working mother; we learned to work together as a family and established a rapport." Any child who expressed an interest in learning to dip chocolate was taught. Four grown daughters now work in the family business. "Our kids understand us because they've been a part of it," says Marie. She talks about several employees who have been working for her for fifteen years as though they, too, are family.

Marie Cavanaugh's daughter Carla now has five children of her own and manages the family's Valley Fair mall kiosk part-time. As Marie says, her daughter has found a way to employ all the women in her church, part-time, so they can all raise their children in the home, while having a way to earn money and some time off for a little adult intellectual stimulation.

The Mihlbergers

Mike Mihlberger grew up in his father's business. Office & Things, his first business venture, was a logical progression of Mike's childhood. His father owned All Makes Typewriter, where Mike worked for nine years sweeping and stamping envelopes. "I grew up not knowing anyone but business people," he says. They became role models. Like most sons, Mike wanted to strike out on his own. "I couldn't stay with Dad forever and feel good about myself." So for six years, Mike worked an assortment of jobs not related to office products. He spent time in college and traveled. When he decided to start his own business, his father provided financial support and encouragement. Mike has turned out to be as "successful an adult" as any parent could hope for.

Why? My theory is that Mike, like Robert and Carla, grew up, like their great-great-grandparents, working and living around their parents and *other* adults. Most children today have only other children to consult if they are dissatisfied with the information their parents provide — verbally or by example. Children are imprisoned in a classroom, then encouraged to spend their after-school hours engaged in extracurricular activities — at school. The few who work, work at fast food places, surrounded by more children their own age, with the same (mis)conceptions about work, money, morals, ethics, etc.

INVOLVING THE CHILDREN

But children involved in the adult workplace have input from many sources. At age thirteen, when parental advice is generally ignored, these children are in daily contact with other adults whose opinions or demands cannot be ignored. They must learn rules of the workplace: timeliness, productivity, personal responsibility, manners, cross-generation social skills, how to treat customers, how to get along with co-workers, etc. Input from parents, co-workers, even customers will mold the adult.

More important, a child can easily make the connection between work done and the "value" of material possessions, when he or she participates in doing the work. The ramifications of an unswept floor in a suburban home are a night alone in one's private room with one's private television set. In a business, the result is a customer who carries a dirty box to the counter and demands a discount for damaged merchandise. Just what, as parents and adults, do we want to teach children?

Even if you start your business after your children have reached their teens or have moved out of your house and are on their own, there are still "family" advantages. Bev Miller purchased Midnight Oil Typesetting from me, as she explained, because she had an eighteen year old who had struggled to finish high school and had some interest in graphic art. For herself, Bev wanted a business to retire into after she took early retirement from her state job. Now she has most of her family employed. "My daughters know it's their business and they get out what they put in," says Bev. Her goal is to move her daughters up to management positions and have others sit at the machines.

PARTNERSHIP

As discussed in a previous chapter, an invaluable employee (in your estimation, not theirs) should be made a partner. The same loyalty exists between members of a family when they all know that they will share equally in the fruits of their labor. Other employees expect (or quickly learn) that the owner will benefit more from success because the owner takes the risks and invests the capital. When the risks and investment (either in dollars or in time) are invested by members of a family, a business gains a longer incubation period, especially if the children live in their parents' house. They'll need less income to meet their needs if they aren't paying rent or house payments.

Jay and Sheri Jensen plan to retire in eight years, when their eldest son, now fifteen, is old enough and "ready to buy them out." They say while their children often complain about their jobs, they complain louder when their parents suggest hiring an outsider to operate the quilting machine. And while fall is a busy time for Jay — the many shows he travels to in nine western states keep him away from home for several months — the family has found that working at home has made them very close and given them ample time to do things together as a family; things that Jay's former job did not accommodate.

If the parents and offspring are all adults — living independently of one another — the dynamics change. The relationship, like any partnership, is subject to the changing needs and expectations of all adults. You and your partner must agree as to the type of business you will start, and you must agree what each person's responsibilities will be. These duties should never overlap. Agree to let each person have the final say over his or her area of responsibility. Discussion, as in all business relationships, is vital. Everyone should share information, but let the bookkeeper keep the books.

Marge (Marguerite) Grossi has been involved with the wedding business for more than thirty years. She started as a seamstress in a shop in upstate New York. She worked her way up into a sales position and received formal training as a bridal consultant. When her husband Al's job brought the family to Salt Lake City, she went to work part-time for Marjorie and Hooper Mortensen, the former owners of The Brides' Shop. They made her manager and, according to Marge's daughter, Kathy Halford, it was the Mortensens who decided that Marge would be the likely candidate to own The Brides' Shop when they retired.

Marge says she never gave owning a shop much serious consideration because she was accustomed to working part-time and having lots of free time to travel. About the time the Mortensens were ready to sell, Al's job took the couple back to New York state. Marge says she kept in touch with the Mortensens and decided she would buy the business and return to Salt Lake after Al retired. Meanwhile, Kathy went to work in The Brides' Shop to become more familiar with the daily operations of the business. Marge and Kathy took over the business in 1983. Mother specializes in selling and serving customers; daughter keeps the books. Since Marge doesn't care for paperwork, the division of labor suits both. Also, Kathy's previous experience working in the advertising department of a local furniture store has enabled her to bring one more skill into the family business.

Their biggest challenge has been to update the store's inventory. Marge's ideas of bridal fashions differ from those of the previous owners. "We've tried to gear ourselves to a more sophisticated woman." To do that, Marge continues to put profits back into the business to expand the inventory. "If you don't have the dresses when the customers come in, you lose them," says Kathy.

Family businesses don't always work out. One of the businesses profiled in this book started out as a father-son-wife/daughter-mother relationship. The in-laws don't speak to one another anymore, probably because of the fact that everyone was trying to run everything. It never works. Not between bosses and employees, business partners, families, even husbands and wives. Don't do it yourselves. Assign duties according to each individual's skills. Then trust that person's judgment. Keep informed; communicate constantly. Look at the books, but don't undo or redo someone else's job. If a family member proves to be incompetent or loses interest, everyone must decide to remove that person from his or her position and find a replacement. But don't try to "fix things" along the way. You'll only fight.

Of all the people I have met who are involved in small business, the ones I have grown to admire most are running, or have been raised in, a family business. These people have an incredible amount of honesty, integrity, and common sense. They are easygoing and realistic, like some of the people I know who were raised on farms.

Small business, while the pay is lower at the outset and the hours often longer than a corporate job, is more humane. It is all right to have both good days and bad days, to have a career and a personal life.

If you want to start a family business, build. Build on your own skills, and put your family's skills to use, too.

14

THE ECONOMY

Running a business is more complicated than you will ever imagine. After years of careful planning, building a loyal clientele and staff, socking away capital for expansion, and finally having a salary that matches your initial expectations, it can all change. You may have made all the right business decisions, but your business's longevity depends on a number of factors that are not in your control: how your suppliers, customers, and landlord operate their businesses, national and local politics, and the economy.

The health of the economy in a city, state, or nation, depends on the amount of cash and credit that is available for the public and private sectors to earn, borrow, and spend. When the economy is good, interest rates are generally low, loans are easy to get, and people borrow a lot of money and spend it on a multitude of real and perceived needs. When the economy is bad, people don't spend; they may or may not save; in fact, they may not even be earning an income to spend or save if they wanted to. The business economy is reflected in the stock market's Dow Jones Index. People's spending habits, coupled with how much faith they have in the future of the country or individual companies, makes the market go up or down. When people *think* things are going badly, they tend not to spend. When they do not spend, businesses go broke; the Dow drops. To some degree, belief and reality are the same thing.

WATCH THE INDICATORS

When the "national indicators," like money supply, interest rates, and the Dow, reflect a bad economy (Bear Market), things are going to be tight for business. Not all business. There are always winners in any recession. But people are less likely to spend money on perceived needs when they are fearful about the future.

As the owner of a business, you must know that good and bad business cycles will occur. You have to save enough in the good cycles to ride out the bad ones. You have another choice: close your business. It is all right to stop.

You are allowed to realize that people are no longer buying what you have to sell, for now or forever, and to stop selling that stuff. But if you are in business for life, for the family, because you cannot imagine working for someone else or doing anything else for a living, save up and ride it out.

Keeping a business alive and profitable requires hard work and an attentive mind. You'd have to have your nose buried deep in your own books not to notice what is going on in the world and how it affects the national economy. Such information is easy to come by, and you can't afford not to pay attention. In addition, a number of social, economic, and political factors will affect the business climate in your state, city, town, even neighborhood. These "factors" comprise the "local economy." The "local economy" is, in part, the impact that money (and credit) has on your environment, your location, the traffic flow into your place of business. The local economy also encompasses "decisions" — specifically, any decision made by someone other than yourself (a business owner) that has an impact on your business.

THE SALT LAKE EXAMPLE

A good example has taken place in Salt Lake City during the past decade. This pattern has happened in many cities, usually over a longer period of time. But Salt Lake is small and because there are fewer businesses in its downtown than in Denver, St. Louis, or New York, change is more noticeable.

About twelve years ago, the city government decided to implement a "beautification program." The plan called for wider sidewalks, decorated with fountains and planters and benches, all of which were installed at the expense of curbside parking. Several years later, developers constructed a second enclosed shopping mall in downtown's Central Business District (CBD). The new mall was built directly across the street from the city's original enclosed mall. "Plans" called for construction of the second mall to be at the south end of the city's CBD, to keep pedestrian traffic on the city's Main Street, where a number of small businesses were located.

Meanwhile the city's Redevelopment Agency designated a major city block as "blighted" and destined for redevelopment. A few long-term residents of the block sued; most small merchants deserted Main Street in favor of the new mall. Corporate decision-making processes prompted JC Penney and F.W. Woolworth's to leave Main Street; both had been located on the Redevelopment Agency's targeted block. The character of Main Street, and downtown Salt Lake, was changed forever. Most pedestrian traffic now travels at the north end of town between the two malls. Merchants on Main Street struggled to survive as owners of older properties sold out or raised their rents to match those of the malls.

My former partner had to relocate when the bank across Main Street purchased the property he rented to construct a new office tower. Fred's neighbor, a shoe store owner, chose to retire early. Fred elected to move across Second South into a space one-third the size, and he had to pay for walls, plumbing, wiring, etc. His sales figures were not high enough at the time to justify that type of expense, because for the previous two years the Main Street renovation project had all but eliminated traffic flow and parking around his block. The move into a smaller, less visible space with virtually no on-street parking proved to be a poor decision.

Salt Lake provides a radical example of change to the "local economy" caused by politics and planning commissions. Chances are, the first you, as a business owner, will hear about these changes is when your landlord notifies you that your lease will not be renewed, or that your rent is going to be raised to match the new "estimated value of downtown commercial real estate."

These numbers are based on "projections" and "estimations" of "future demand for prime property." In other words, the city politicians and bureaucrats think more and more people are going to move into the area and fill up all the new buildings that developers and bankers are creating in their town. What the politicians and landlords never tell you about is the two to five years it is going to take before the construction is completed, the detour signs come down, and the public (your customers) can, once again, get to your place of business.

BE POLITICALLY AWARE

The point is: keep an eye on city hall. Find out what is going on in the city/town/neighborhood where you have your business. If most of your customers park in the lot behind your store, and someone builds an apartment building there, as also happened to Fred, that should tell you something. Pay attention. In Salt Lake, people are accustomed to parking in front of their destination. New Yorkers walk everywhere and consider themselves lucky if they find a parking space on the island on Manhattan. When parking is expensive and public transportation adequate, maybe Salt Lake will become a pedestrian city. But the successful businesses there realize that is not now the case; and every business, city council, or public policy meeting centers around the issue of adequate parking and making the city accessible to the automobile.

While I walked a mile and a half to work everyday, I had to be honest about my world. When I located Midnight Oil Typesetting in an out-of-the-way building with a parking lot, I did better than when I was in the heart of town with no parking.

In the first five years, you may be too busy to pay attention to politics. But you cannot afford not to. Believe half the rumors you hear, then make phone calls to those who really know: the Chamber of Commerce, your legislators and city or county officials, planning and zoning people ...

THE DANGER OF MALLS

If you are located in a shopping mall, the danger is double. You not only risk city political projections and renovations, you are at the mercy of the whims of mall management. Remember: Mall management's job is to *collect rent* from you. The marketing director may talk a lot about helping your business grow and succeed. The musical entertainment that takes place during Christmas in the center court is an effort on behalf of every tenant to attract traffic to the mall. Your merchants' association dues pay for this. Don't forget it. The mall's owners consider you a renter. To the extent the company makes money from your business, management is interested in your welfare. That means that national chains are more interesting than small start-up companies.

Just as the national economy has cycles, so do malls. Two things happen frequently: malls change ownership, and malls renovate. If a new company purchases the mall where you rent space, find out what their plans are. Ask for a long-term lease. If they say no, find out why. Renovation is a bigger danger than change of ownership, but renovation often follows a change in ownership. Even malls that don't change owners are likely to renovate, and the period for change is typically twelve years.

If the mall plans to renovate and, say, move you upstairs, ask who will pay for the move. Unless you have a long-term lease, you may have to, and your rent will increase, because what management is going to do will "improve traffic flow into the mall, so your space will be worth more," or some such thinking. Really? Don't take their word for it or depend on mall management to help you succeed. They have only one real purpose, and that is to collect rent — the same as the landlord in the building you leased on Main Street. If the renovation plans don't attract pedestrian traffic, they will not apologize, explain, or lower your rent right away. Remember, landlords are just landlords. And while it is true that malls do more group advertising and sponsor more events than main streets, you pay for it in higher rents and in most cases, tenant association dues.

Meanwhile, just like those Salt Lake businesses on Main Street, you will have to put up with dust and scaffolding and, even worse, reduced traffic flow past your shop during remodeling. Why? People don't like to climb around building materials, and when malls renovate, they tend also to raise rents and make tenants move to different locations within the mall. This means a lot of your neighbors are going to move out or close down. Fewer stores will be in the mall for a while (years), and fewer shoppers.

Should you stick it out anyway? If your business depends on a regular clientele for 80% or more of your income, and those people are so loyal that they are going to cope with dust, yes. But if you are selling an item that people are likely to buy only if they are in the vicinity, no way. People won't put up with too much inconvenience to get to your pizza snack bar. There are too many around to patronize instead. They might go through a little trouble to patronize your high fashion boutique, if you sell the only clothing of its kind in your area.

Consider why your neighbors are staying or leaving once the renovation/rearrangement has been announced. A national store can draw funds from the parent company to pay bills for the year(s) it will take the mall to finish the changes. If you are operating a small start-up company, you'll still have the same fixed costs of doing business: rent, utilities, pre-paid advertising. You can cut staff, if sales fall. But what about inventory? Are your customers used to seeing your gift shop packed with merchandise? Will they still come in if you cut back? A quick-print shop in a mall can easily stock less paper. It takes a day or two to get delivery of paper from the distributor. But if you are in the business of selling quantity and variety, it will be hard to convince your customers that they should settle for less choice during the renovation. They are likely to go elsewhere. And when demand picks up, can you restock quickly if your merchandise comes from California or New York and takes three months to arrive?

MOVING

Moving, to some extent, is starting over. You'll have to spend a lot for store remodeling; you may have to decrease your inventory to fit your new space or your available working capital.

Moving can be beneficial. Trust your own research, not someone else's promises. Guy, The Ringmaker, was promised high foot traffic past his original mall location. It did not happen; but he survived long enough to move to a better spot in the same mall. Other merchants in his "corridor" were not so fortunate. Some are still in business and prospering, like Mike's office supply shop. Since the original fiasco on Main Street, rents have fallen in response to supply and (lack of) demand. Eric opened a second Edinburgh Castle on Main Street. He says rents are lower and traffic higher than seventeen years ago when his wife, Betty, first owned the lingerie shop on the same street, before the malls were built. Then again, where else can people go for bagpipes and kilts? The jewelers and optical shops have all but abandoned Main Street in favor of mall locations. Comparison shopping habits and validated parking work in their favor.

Another factor that will affect your local economy is competition. Consider how many other businesses like yours have opened since you started. If there are many, people can go elsewhere if your store becomes inconvenient to get to during a renovation. If there are few, people will have to make the effort.

Your first reaction to a potential renovation or forced move may be to relocate to another mall or back to Main Street. Again, consider why people shop in your place of business. If they impulse-buy your chocolate candy, for example, when they come to the mall to buy clothing, they probably won't travel to a second mall just to seek you out. If they shop at your store exclusively but live in a different part of the city or state, having your business move into their neighborhood might bring you even more business. Better yet, open a branch like Judy's Classy Lady, or Marie and George's Mrs. Cavanaugh's Candies.

Are your customers walkers or commuters? How important is storefront parking? Access? Visibility? Before change happens to you, you must consider all these things. You must find out who your customers are and why they patronize your business. To find this out, ask. Surveys and questionnaires are a start, but you are limiting your information to those people who are willing to be surveyed or to fill out and mail your questionnaire. This information is too limited and too late. Find out as much as you can from your customers every time they visit your store. Engage in conversations. Ask as many people, as casually as possible, why they come to you. Then you will know what you need to know when the local economy forces you to make a change.

TECHNOLOGY

Another aspect of "local economy" is changing technology. As discussed before, just when you think you have built a loyal clientele, and you almost have your computer system paid for, a competitor will move into the neighborhood with the newest machine that produces twice as much at half the cost. Do you hold your ground? Reduce prices? Update your equipment? Again, the first decision you must make is how badly you want to continue in the same line of work (that is: self employment). Put pencil to paper and figure out how many years it will take to recoup your investment if you upgrade. Better still, consider leasing if you are in a technologically sensitive business. Or make certain that you purchase hardware that will be able to handle whatever new software becomes available, so that you can upgrade your system at a minimal cost. The reason to change is never "to match the competition." The reason to change your business, retool your machinery, or purchase a new computer system is the same reason you started a business in the first place — to make money. If you can't or it will take too many years to recover your investment before you turn a profit, consider a different course. Keep doing what you are doing until your business is no longer able to operate at a profit. Don't let yourself get into debt or bankruptcy. Simply pay attention to the bottom line, try to hold your market share, and if that erodes substantially, stop. Just stop — that means go out of business. Sound gloomy? Not at all.

THE ENTREPRENEURIAL PROFILE

Scratch the surface of any successful business person and you are likely to find someone who has owned a number of businesses — some successful, some not. Eric and Betty Gilzean owned a custom lingerie shop. Betty started in the custom-fitted bra business with a home-marketing company. Eventually the Gilzeans purchased the factory in California and opened their retail store in Salt Lake. Betty operated the lingerie shop and Eric worked as an independent painting contractor. Eric says he got interested in retail when he started to do his wife's books. He learned that she was making more money than he was. So he started to work in her shop doing ordering and record keeping. Eventually the couple opened outlets in several suburban shopping malls.

Their successful venture into lingerie enabled the Gilzeans to pursue the idea of opening a Scottish imports store with vigor and sufficient capital. By 1986, the couple had closed the last of their Betty's Bra Bar locations, and concentrated all their efforts on Edinburgh Castle. Since 20% of their business is already done over the telephone, Eric says their next change will be expanding into mail order.

Another business owner who turned a change in the local economy into a new business idea is Wayne Scott, president of Carriage Horse Livery. He was working in the construction business and breeding race horses when the demand for new housing suddenly took a nose dive.

Wayne had worked on a cattle ranch in Idaho when he was young and recalls using draft horses and bobsleds to take feed to the cattle in the winter. When he moved to Salt Lake to build a housing project, Wayne purchased a team of Clydesdales and a Schwartz Vis-a-Vis (face-to-face) carriage to take prospective clients around the property.

On a business trip in 1983, Wayne says he overheard a flight attendant complain that Salt Lake City's downtown folds up after dark. At the time, the real estate market was beginning to suffer from a glut of builders and too few buyers. Wayne wanted to find a "more wholesome" atmosphere in which to raise his children than the race horse circuit. So, he applied for a temporary permit and after eighteen months, got permission from the City Council to take his horses and carriages on the street to sell rides. After three years he built his business to 10 carriages, 18 to 20 horses, a horse-drawn trolley, sleigh rides, and hay rides. Employees have been easy to find, as horse lovers simply find the place and ask for work.

Finding horses that will adapt to work on city streets is the hardest part of the job, says Wayne. They not only have to adapt to city noises, but must learn to respond to voice commands. "Four in a thousand" meet the criteria. When I first interviewed Wayne, in May 1988, he said ten carriages were as many as the city could accommodate. However, after he had built his business to that level of service, a competitor entered the arena. Following his own advice, Wayne chose to diversify his services and offer horse and carriage rides in other places. So he obtained the concessions at several state parks.

Still, the logical end to one business led nicely to the birth of a second. Entrepreneurs are like that. While you will certainly grow to love (or hate) your successful business, what you will find is that being in business for yourself is what really matters. The product or service you offer is secondary. The real entrepreneur will adapt to changing market conditions by upgrading, expanding, buying, leasing, selling, hiring, firing, raising or lowering prices ... whatever it takes to remain ethical, profitable, and in business. And if those efforts are either not affordable or simply too distasteful, the real entrepreneur will close one shop and find another to open that will be more suited to the times.

Just as Clair and Twila changed The Ink Spot from a print shop and office supply business into office supplies and Hallmark cards, and Mike dropped specialty gifts in favor of stuffed animals, so should you change your business to respond to changes in the local economy. Even Midnight Oil Typesetting, with its updated technology and method of operation, is a different business than the one I owned and operated. I used to spend as much time visiting with my customers as I ever spent typesetting. Bev Miller and family run a more "business-like" operation. Theirs is a drop-it-off and pick-it-up later system. Mine was a sit-and-visit and I'll do your work while you wait and we talk business. It seems I was always taking notes for a book I did not know I would write. But here it is.

THE CHANGING TIMES

Certain types of businesses will survive major changes in the local economy. The nation's passion for chocolate seems to keep candy companies in business for generations. It is likely that we will be sending greeting cards through the mail for a long, long time to come. The messages may change, but the business will remain viable, I would guess, until postage stamps cost more than people are willing to pay ($1.00? $5.00?) and every household in America and the world is able to communicate electronically by personal computer for less than the cost of a stamp. Still, greeting cards have the advantage of providing a preprinted message that someone else — a poet or copywriter — wrote. Perhaps Hallmark will sell floppy disks that you can insert in your computer, then you'll select an appropriate greeting, and send it over the modem. Clair and Twila's and Robert's descendants are likely to be operating a different type of business than the Hales are now.

There is only one absolute truth about business: CHANGE. Times change, tastes change, employees change, you will change, and your business will change if it is to survive. Think about some things that you have purchased regularly your entire life. Even the products in a grocery store have multiplied in quantity and variety. Consider eyeglasses and hairstyles. One Salt Lake optical shop is now run by a third generation. The business is the same, but the products and method of operation have changed. Frame styles come in designer labels. Contact lenses can even change the color of your eyes or correct your vision. Standard Optical built a lab that custom makes lenses in an hour now; even five years ago, it took a week or two.

Hairdressing has changed. The world is no longer divided into beauty shops for women and barber shops for men; although both still exist. Nowadays, styling salons cater to both sexes, and men's and women's hairstyles look ever more alike. In the '60s, hippies simply let their hair grow long. Today's trendsetters have "hair styles." Someone has to cut it that way, spray it to stand on end, dye it pink.

So, count on change, plan for it, save for it, and decide what you are going to do when it happens: adapt, evolve, or stop. The true entrepreneur does not want to work for someone else. You will find some way to avoid the regular hours, the three-piece suit, the punch cards and regular paychecks. You will want to take responsibility for your income, your hours, your work, your successes and failures. You may even be motivated by the idea of never having to wear another suit or attend another company party. Or maybe you are a dreamer, like me. My dream is never to have to ask another person to stop talking, playing the radio, or whatever, while I write. I want control over my environment: no smoking, no noise. My goal is to use my time and abilities to good purpose. I want to write things for people to read; not put in file folders. With the profits, I want to buy art and help animals.

Whatever your dream, I wish you the best.

Appendices

1. CHECKLIST FOR GOING INTO BUSINESS

Before you start your business, ask yourself these questions. The more "yes" answers you check, the more prepared you are to open and operate a business successfully.

Yes No **You:**

❑ ❑ I am self-motivated, able to initiate projects and carry them through.

❑ ❑ I have good social skills and can interact well with people.

❑ ❑ When I initiate a project, other people willingly help me to complete it.

❑ ❑ I enjoy responsibility.

❑ ❑ I am organized and can devise a plan of action that others will follow in order to accomplish mutual goals.

❑ ❑ I am willing to work as long, as hard, or as smart, as is necessary to get the job done.

❑ ❑ I am able to make decisions quickly, and accept the consequences of those decisions.

❑ ❑ I am honest. I don't keep secrets and I tell the truth. I will share business information with my employees so we can build an effective team ("family").

❑ ❑ Once I've decided to accomplish something, I can be flexible about the strategy, but remain set upon the goal.

❑ ❑ The goals I set for myself and others are reasonable and achievable.

❑ ❑ I have experience in a business or hobby similar to the one I plan to start.

❑ ❑ I have enough money saved to pay my bills while I get my business off the ground.

❑ ❑ My education has prepared me for the business I plan to start.

Money:

❑ ❑ I have estimated the amount of money I will need to start my business.

❑ ❑ I have money of my own (savings) to invest in my business.

❑ ❑ I have made arrangements to borrow the rest of the money I need from friends, family, banks, etc.

❑ ❑ I have contacted my suppliers and know which ones will demand cash payments and which ones will extend me a line of credit.

❑ ❑ I have calculated how much income (salary plus year-end profit) I can expect to make from my business, if any, during the first five years.

❑ ❑ I will be able to reinvest some of my earnings back into the business to help it grow during the start-up years.

❑ ❑ Based on my sales projections, income generated by the business will be sufficient to pay business expenses and service any debt.

Partner (if applicable):

❑ ❑ My business partner and I communicate well and have agreed on our respective areas of responsibility.

❑ ❑ I trust my partner to manage his/her responsibilities and, in return, I have his/her trust.

❑ ❑ My partner and I have complementary business skills and financial resources.

❑ ❑ We have written and signed a partnership agreement that clearly defines our business, our relationship and responsibilities, and our mutual goals.

Customers:

❑ ❑ The economy in the town I plan to start my business is in good shape.

❑ ❑ The people who live here earn a good living and can afford my product or service; or there are many businesses in this community that have both the need and the budget for my product or service.

❑ ❑ My product or service will compete well in this marketplace.

❑ ❑ The kind of people who are likely to buy my product or service live or work near my store location; or my product/service is so unusual that people will be willing to travel some distance to get it (or order by mail).

❑ ❑ My product or service is needed in this community by the people who live or work here.

❑ ❑ Stores similar to mine are doing well in my community and in the rest of the country.

❑ ❑ My prices, service, and quality will attract and keep customers.

❑ ❑ My customers will have sufficient reason to return to my store and make purchases on a regular basis.

❑ ❑ I will be able to resolve customers' complaints to their satisfaction.

❑ ❑ I will be able to service and repair things I sell (if necessary).

❑ ❑ I have a (written and posted) return policy and satisfaction guarantee.

❑ ❑ My customers will have ample reason to recommend my store to their friends and acquaintances, and business associates.

Location:

❑ ❑ I have found a location for my business that will make it easy for my customers to find and patronize my business.

❑ ❑ This location will be able to accommodate my business as it grows.

❑ ❑ The amount of money necessary to renovate/reconstruct my business location is within my budget and means.

❑ ❑ My place of business is easy to get to from a parking lot or space, bus stops, or homes and businesses.

❑ ❑ My business complies with local zoning (health and fire) regulations.

❑ ❑ I understand the terms and conditions of my lease and they are reasonable.

Equipment and Supplies:

❑ ❑ I have made a list of the equipment and supplies I will need to operate my business and I have contacted suppliers to determine how much they will cost. (Make a list.)

Product or Service:

❑ ❑ I have decided what I will sell.

❑ ❑ I have compared prices and credit terms of different suppliers.

❑ ❑ I have found suppliers who will sell me what I need at a good price and will deliver same on time, as promised.

❑ ❑ I will have an ample supply of merchandise (retail), materials (manufacturing), or supplies (service) on hand when I open for business.

❑ ❑ I have made arrangements to reorder supplies/merchandise/materials in order to keep my business in continuous operation — my customers will have ample merchandise to choose from and/or I will be able to fill orders as promised.

Record Keeping:

❑ ❑ I have a record keeping system that will keep me apprised of how much I earn, what and to whom I owe money, who owes me money, and by when debts are to be paid and receivables collected.

❑ ❑ I will have enough to sell and service my customers' needs, but not more.

❑ ❑ I have a record keeping system for payroll, and tax reports and payments.

❑ ❑ I have an accountant.

Legal Matters:

❏ ❏ I have obtained all the business licenses and permits I need.

❏ ❏ I know (or have) an attorney who can advise me on relevant business law.

❏ ❏ I have filed all the necessary forms with federal, state, and local government agencies, and know what is expected on a periodic basis.

Security:

❏ ❏ I have sufficient security to protect my business from shoplifting, robbery, burglary, and employee theft.

❏ ❏ I have adequate insurance coverage for my business, my employees, my customers, and myself.

Advertising:

❏ ❏ I have a plan and a budget for advertising.

❏ ❏ I have obtained advertising rate information from the media (TV, radio, newspapers, magazines) and have received bids on printing flyers, brochures, and promotional materials.

❏ ❏ I have obtained demographic data from the media so I can determine which ones reach my target audience.

❏ ❏ I have decided to advertise in the same manner as my competition; or to position myself in the marketplace by selecting alternate venues.

❏ ❏ My advertising campaign will successfully encourage customers to choose my business over the competition.

❏ ❏ I have determined whether or not it will be necessary to conduct "special sales" in order to compete effectively in my marketplace.

❏ ❏ I have chosen a professional who can help me devise an appropriate advertising and promotional campaign.

Prices:

❏ ❏ My prices reflect all of my costs (costs of goods sold, fixed and variable expenses, overhead) plus a reasonable return on investment (profit).

❏ ❏ I know what my competitors charge.

❏ ❏ My prices are competitive; or my prices are higher than the competition, but my service and quality will justify the difference and be readily apparent to my customers.

Buying:

❏ ❏ I will find out (ask, survey) what my customers want.

❏ ❏ My inventory system will tell me when it is time to reorder and how much I should buy.

❏ ❏ My suppliers have an interest in my success.

Selling:

❏ ❏ I have decided whether or not I will need employees (outside my immediate family).

❏ ❏ I have chosen a method by which to find employees (classified ad, placement service, referrals, recruitment).

❏ ❏ I have set salaries and wages that will attract the most qualified and dedicated people.

❏ ❏ I have a plan for training my employees.

❏ ❏ I have a plan for rewarding excellent performance, and will be as quick to compliment as to correct.

❏ ❏ I will not hesitate to terminate an incompetent or dishonest employee, even though firing people can be hard to do.

❏ ❏ I will have a written policy for my employees so they understand the goals and objectives of my business and can participate in same, and so they will understand their duties and responsibilities, wages and benefits.

❏ ❏ I will be available to discuss ideas, suggestions, observations, concerns, and problems with my employees, so we can work together to make this business a success.

❏ ❏ I will earn my employees' respect, not demand it as a condition of employment.

❏ ❏ I will expect excellence from my employees and will provide them with the products, prices, training, and environment that will motivate them, in turn, to do their best for me.

Customer Credit:

❏ ❏ I have decided whether or not to let customers buy on credit. If so, I have designed a credit application, which will determine the difference between good credit risks and deadbeats.

❏ ❏ I have investigated the pros and cons of providing credit card service for my customers.

❏ ❏ My customers understand when payment is due because they have been told and provided with a written copy of credit terms for any sale that is not cash-and-carry.

2. REGISTER YOUR BUSINESS NAME

By registering your business name with the state, you receive a protected right to its use — other businesses in your marketing area, offering services similar to yours, may not use the same (or a similar) name.

Anyone may use his or her proper name as his or her business name. There is no limit to the number of Susie Madden Bookstores allowed in your town as long as everyone who owns one of those stores is named Susie Madden. On the other hand, if your bookstore is named Stargazer, that same name could be used for the title of a magazine or a car wash in your town, or a bookstore in another (non-competing) town either in your state or another state.

Registering your business name does not give you trademark, copyright, or patent protection. Those protections, obtainable from the federal government, give you exclusive right to the use of your business or product name for a period of time. No others can use it.

The state requires that you register your business name for your protection and the protection of other businesses and consumers. Anyone can call the state and find out who owns a business using an assumed name.

What will happen if you fail to register? It could cost you a lot of money, for one thing. As owner of Midnight Oil Typesetting, I had a number of customers who had called the state to find out if anyone else had registered the business name they wanted to use. Several received a preliminary go-ahead from the state. So they bought business stationery. When the official form arrived in the mail, they found out someone else had already registered that name. Hundreds of dollars later, each one chose a different business name, registered it, and reprinted newly designed and typeset letterhead, envelopes, and business cards. Telephone calls are inadequate. What the state tells you on the phone may be inaccurate.

If your name is not registered, and someone else registers it (even years later), the state will ask you to stop using the name. Why lose all the name recognition you've built over the years because of an oversight on paperwork? Actually, it's hard to miss this one, since your local government will ask you for your registered name (DBA) when you apply for a business name. Nevertheless, wait until you receive official — written — notification from the state before you spend any money on signs, brochures, stationery, and business forms.

3. NEW BUSINESS COMPLIANCE CHECKLIST

Registration of a Business Name

All persons or partnerships doing business under an assumed name must register with the state.

State Business License

Under certain circumstances, a special state business license may be required for your business. Usually, only professionals need a state business license, i.e., CPA's, doctors, construction companies, etc.

City/County Business License

Business licenses may or may not be required by cities or counties throughout the state. Contact your local city or county office for details.

Federal Employer's Tax I.D. Number

Every person without a previous tax number who pays wages to one or more employee or is required to file any federal reports must apply for a tax number on Form SS-4 with the IRS.

Federal Tax Information

Contact the IRS for information related to income, excise, self-employment, and other federal taxes. The IRS also provides a Business Tax Kit and Tax Seminar for businesses. The seminar will provide you with basic instructions and forms for reporting federal taxes on your business.

Minimum Wage Laws

Many businesses are subject to federal minimum wage, overtime, and child labor law regulations. For information, contact the U.S. Department of Labor, Wage, Hour and Public Contracts Division.

State Employer's Tax I.D. Number

Information concerning applications for a state tax number may be obtained from the State Tax Commission.

State Tax Information

For information related to income tax, sales and use taxes, and other applicable state taxes, contact the State Tax Commission.

Unemployment Insurance

Unemployment insurance, both state and federal, is generally required in firms with one or more employee. For information contact the Department of Employment Security.

Worker's Compensation Insurance

Worker's Compensation Insurance is required of all employers. This insurance may be obtained from private insurance companies or the State Insurance Fund. For information contact the State Industrial Commission.

Zoning

Contact your local zoning office to ensure that your business location is properly zoned for commercial use.

Property Taxes

Property taxes are levied on land, building, and equipment used in a business. For information, contact the County Assessor.

Bulk Sales Act

When purchasing a business, the purchaser is potentially subject to liability for all debts of the acquired business. Compliance with the Bulk Sales Act is a means of limiting this liability. Seek competent legal advice in order to comply with this act.

4. CONTRACTS

Do not copy these contract documents and use them for your business. If these documents have any legal value it is only because they were, in fact, negotiated (over a period of hours or days), then written and signed by the parties involved. In other words, we agreed in mind and in writing. That, I believe, is the definition of a contract. But my contracts copied for your situation may not fulfill that criteria.

Why, therefore, are these documents included in this book? Because they will give you an idea of the points to ponder (and discuss) when starting, buying, or selling a business.

Would these documents stand up in court? I don't know; I've never had to find out. In fact, most were filed permanently in my drawer (until now), because I had no further need for them.

I did use my original partnership agreement. When I pointed out to my partner the fact that he was not fulfilling his obligations under the terms of our original agreement, I convinced him to sign the partnership dissolution agreement. We didn't need an attorney. We had both agreed to all the terms and conditions of that original contract, and when Fred changed his mind, I was able to convince him that he was no longer acting as my "partner," so he should simply go his own way. This conversation actually lasted six months. But he agreed. We split the equipment and went our separate ways.

I have written other agreements as needed in my writing business. I don't expect I will ever have to test any of my contracts in court. I am certain the thought and discussion that preceded writing each one is sufficient to make the signatories live up to the terms therein.

PARTNERSHIP AGREEMENT

THIS AGREEMENT made and entered into this 30th day of November, 1979, by and between FRED BLACKBURN, hereinafter called "Blackburn," and JOYCE MARDER, hereinafter called "Marder."

1. PURPOSE. It is the purpose and mutual understanding of the parties hereto that the purpose for creating a partnership is to have two partners who are familiar with and who are able to operate the business in the absence of the other partner. Any sale to a third party should be made to a person who is likewise able to operate the business, and who is familiar with the typing and typesetting equipment.

2. NAME AND ADDRESS. The parties hereby form a partnership to carry on, under the name of "Midnight Oil," a typesetting business, which business shall include typesetting and other printing preparation services in Salt Lake County, Utah, and elsewhere, as the parties may from time to time

determine. The initial business address of the partnership shall be at 165 South West Temple, Suite 300-C, Salt Lake City, Utah 84111.

3.   TERM. The partnership shall be deemed to have begun retroactively as of July 1, 1979, and shall continue from year to year, unless there shall be delivered to either partner by the other of them a written notification of his or her intention to dissolve the partnership.

4.   CAPITAL. Blackburn currently owns certain equipment which is to be or which already has been contributed to the partnership, including one IBM Selectric Composer, and IBM Memory Typewriter, a Strip Printer and Strip Printer Fonts, a Dictaphone 180 System, current files, a light table, and miscellaneous supplies. The business was and is an ongoing enterprise prior to the formation of the partnership and was solely owned and operated by Blackburn.

For the sum of Eight Thousand Dollars ($8,000.00), in hand paid, it is mutually agreed by and between the parties that Marder shall own 49% of the equipment and good will of the business, and that Blackburn shall own 51% of the equipment and good will of the business. It is further understood and agreed that Marder will own 49% of all of the assets of the business, including fixed assets, customer lists and the lease, and that Blackburn will own 51% of all assets of the business, including fixed assets, customer lists and the lease.

The parties further agree that of the Eight Thousand Dollars ($8,000.00) paid to Blackburn for a 49% interest in said business, the sum of $1,000.00 shall remain in the savings account herewith created, to be used by the parties as working capital of the partnership. The parties also agree that any attorney fees incurred in connection with the creation of this partnership shall be paid from the $8,000.00 paid to Blackburn.

5.   LOCATION OF BUSINESS. The business is currently located at 165 South West Temple, Suite 300-C, Salt Lake City, Utah 84111. The parties agree that said business shall be furnished with adequate supplies of paper and typesetting cartridges, pens, pencils, tape and other supplies for the business to operate as usual for a period of ninety (90) days without any further expenditures for supplies. After the initial ninety (90) day period, all supplies shall be purchased from income derived from the operation of the business. The ninety day period shall be deemed to have commenced as of July 1, 1979, the date of the creation of the partnership.

6.   TYPESETTING RATES. Typesetting rates shall be set at twenty dollars ($20.00) per hour to begin. Any price increases in the typesetting rates shall be mutually agreed upon by the partners.

Blackburn agrees that all typesetting required by PIP 43 and PIP 303, or any other PIP franchises owned or operated by Blackburn in the Salt Lake Metropolitan Area shall be contracted out to "Midnight Oil."

Should any PIP franchises owned by Blackburn be sold to third parties, Blackburn agrees to make appropriate arrangements in any buy-sell agreement (a) to guarantee continued contracting of business for typesetting services with "Midnight Oil," or (b) to justly compensate Marder, her heirs or assigns, for any loss of business caused thereby.

7. DEATH OF PARTNER. In the event of the death of either partner, the surviving partner has first option to purchase the deceased partner's share of the partnership using the formula for determining the value of the deceased partner's interest as set forth in paragraph 8 hereafter. In the event that the surviving partner waives his right of first option, the heirs of the deceased partner may elect to sell the deceased partner's interest to another party, in which case such sale shall be with the consent of the surviving partner in order that a working relationship may exist.

8. SALE OF PARTNER'S SHARE TO THIRD PARTIES. Should either Blackburn or Marder desire to sell his or her share of the partnership, the other partner shall have the right of first refusal to purchase the same. The purchase price shall not be more than the selling partner's interest in said partnership as determined by the following formula: The value of the partnership for the purposes of this agreement at any given point in time shall be deemed to be Twenty Thousand Dollars ($20,000.00), together with interest thereon at the rate of fifteen percent (15%) per annum from and after July 1, 1979, plus the actual cost of equipment purchase for the business from and after January 1, 1980. If the terms of sale are not cash, then any other terms of sale must be mutually agreeable to both parties.

In the event that either partner does not elect to exercise his right of first refusal, and does not in fact purchase his partner's share of the partnership, then, and in that event, the partner desiring to sell his interest in the partnership shall have the right to sell the same to a third party at a price which shall not be less favorable than was offered to the other partner.

Notwithstanding any other provisions herein, in the event that Blackburn should die, or desire to sell his interest in the partnership, Marder shall have the option to buy two percent of the partnership interest from Blackburn's 51% upon payment to Blackburn or his heirs of the value of such 2% interest based upon the formula stated above.

9. SALARY. Marder shall be operating partner and shall manage the business of the partnership. The partners agree that Marder shall take a draw from the gross income of the business receipts based upon the following schedule:

Gross Income/Month	Draw/Month
$1,200 - $1,500	$800.00/month
$1,500 - $2,500	$900.00/month
$2,500 - up	$1,000.00/month

Marder shall be entitled to also receive 49% of the net profits and Blackburn shall be entitled to receive 51% of the net profits from the operation of the business, the same to be divided between the partners within fifteen (15) days after the end of each calendar quarter.

10.   VACATION. Marder shall be entitled to one week's paid vacation per year beginning in 1980. Marder shall also be entitled to one week's leave or unpaid vacation per year, and during any paid or unpaid vacation as set forth herein, Blackburn or another party suitable to the partners shall perform all typesetting and other work required to run the business so that the continuity of the business is not disrupted.

Marder shall be entitled to any unused but earned vacation time from her employment with PIP prior to the effective date of this partnership agreement, in addition to any vacation time set forth above.

11.   OTHER EMPLOYEES. After the business grosses $3,000.00 per month for at least three consecutive months, and after indications are that no additional profits can be realized without addition of other employees, the partners agree then and in that event that additional employees shall be paid in accordance with the amount of additional business that said employee generates (e.g., any gross income received over and above $3,000.00 per month generated, which is a result of said employee's efforts).

Temporary help may be employed if seasonal fluctuations in the business so indicate or if they are required to maintain customer service and/or customer relations.

12.   ADVERTISING. The partners agree that two percent (2%) of the gross income shall be set aside and may be utilized for advertising purposes. Any unused portion of those funds which are set aside for advertising purposes shall be divided between Blackburn and Marder on a 51/49 basis at the end of the calendar year.

13.   TERMS OF TRADE. PIP 43 and PIP 303 may not resell typesetting performed by Midnight Oil at a higher mark-up. Midnight Oil may arrange for trading or exchanging of its typesetting service or printing service with PIP 43 or PIP 303 at fair market value. Typesetting performed for any other PIP franchises, other than those in which Blackburn has an interest, must be sold at a higher rate than those sold to PIP 43 or PIP 303, or other PIP franchises in which Blackburn has an interest.

14.   REINVESTMENT OF PROFITS. Four percent (4%) of the gross income shall be reinvested into the business as working capital, until the working capital reaches a level of $8,000.00, or whatever other sum the partners shall jointly agree upon in writing. All working capital is to be held in a joint savings account, and is to be withdrawn only upon the signature of both partners.

15.   PURCHASE OF NEW EQUIPMENT. Any working capital may be used with joint written approval of the partners for the purchase of new equipment, as both partners may deem necessary, and as the efficient operation of the business may require.

16.   LOSSES. All losses in the business and all indebtedness to creditors of the business shall be borne on a 51/49 split between Blackburn and Marder. General expenses of the business shall be deducted before any computation of net partnership profits is made.

17.   BOOKS. Partnership books shall be maintained at the principal office of the partnership and each partner shall at all times have access thereto. The books of the partnership shall be kept on a calendar year. At the request of either partner, but at the expense of the partnership, an audit may be made at the end of each calendar year by an outside independent public accountant.

18.   BANKING. All funds of the partnership shall be deposited in its name in such checking account or accounts as shall be designated by the partners. All withdrawals therefrom shall be made upon checks signed by either partner.

19.   DISSOLUTION. Upon the dissolution of the partnership for any cause, an inventory, at market value, shall be taken of the equipment and supplies on hand, and an accounting of all transactions of the business shall be had, and after paying or discharging or providing for all partnership obligations, the remaining assets shall be divided upon a 51/49 basis split between Blackburn and Marder, their heirs or assigns. The provisions of this paragraph shall not supersede the provisions of paragraphs six and seven above.

20.   ARBITRATION. In the event of a disagreement with respect to any matter arising out of this agreement or with respect to the conduct of the partnership business, or in the event of any controversy arising hereunder, such disagreement or controversy shall be settled by arbitration in accordance with the rules of the American Arbitration Association and judgment upon the award rendered may be entered in any court of law having jurisdiction thereof.

21.   BREACH. In the event of breach of this agreement by any of the parties hereto, and in the event that such party is not required by the other party to seek arbitration, then, and in that event, said wronged party may seek legal redress, and if successful, shall be entitled to his costs, and a reasonable attorney's fee.

     IN WITNESS WHEREOF: the parties have signed this agreement on the date first written:

DISSOLUTION OF PARTNERSHIP AGREEMENT
MIDNIGHT OIL TYPESETTING

WHEREAS, Fred Blackburn (Blackburn) has stated his intention to no longer participate in Midnight Oil Typesetting ("Midnight Oil," "the business") as outlined in the Partnership Agreement between Blackburn and Joyce Marder (Marder) dated 30 November 1979, it is the intention of Marder to gain sole ownership of Midnight Oil.

In paragraph 1, PURPOSE, of aforementioned agreement, the purpose of the partnership between Blackburn and Marder was to "have two partners who are familiar with and who are able to operate the business in the absence of the other partner." Paragraph 10, VACATION, states that "Marder shall be entitled to one week's paid vacation per year ... during any paid or unpaid vacation as set forth herein, Blackburn or another party suitable to the partners shall perform all typesetting and other work required to run the business so that the continuity of the business is not disrupted."

Since Blackburn has not participated for over six months in the business by operating the business as had been customary during the first year and one-half of operation on Marder's day off, and since Blackburn has stated that he does not intend (is unable) to operate the business when Marder takes her vacation in 1982 and thereafter, and since no funds are available to hire any other person to do so, it appears that the intent of the partnership agreement has been breached. Since Blackburn is legally entitled to a fifty-one percent (51%) share of any profits of Midnight Oil, it has been the custom and understanding of Marder that Blackburn would do his share of the work, namely typesetting, getting business, providing accounting records. Blackburn has done nothing for over six months.

Since Blackburn has also sold his interest in the PIP (X-Press) Printing stores and therefore no longer contributes directly or indirectly to the future of Midnight Oil, Marder feels that she should no longer be under any obligation to share any profits of the business with Blackburn.

At the time Blackburn and Marder wrote the Partnership Agreement they set terms for SALE OF PARTNER'S SHARE. The value of Midnight Oil was projected to be $20,000.00 assuming that business would continue in the customary manner and that Midnight Oil would increase its income and profitability. Since the beginning of 1981, this projection has proven untrue. In fact, Midnight Oil has operated at a breakeven level for the majority of the year 1981 and the net profit for the year was substantially less than the net profit for 1980. Therefore, Marder feels that the true value of Midnight Oil is the depreciated value of the assets of the business and her personal ability to generate future business. Furthermore, Blackburn no longer contributes in any way to the future profitability of Midnight Oil.

Since mid-1981, Blackburn has neglected to provide Marder with sales figures for typesetting done for X-Press Printing. Blackburn has also failed to pay Midnight Oil for typesetting work done for Blackburn, specifically coupons, as well as several hundred dollars worth of typesetting done for the 21st South store (no longer in existence) and the 2nd South store for which no records were kept or provided for several months prior to Blackburn's selling the print shops.

In consideration of the aforesaid conditions, the partnership between Blackburn and Marder is hereby dissolved as of April 1, 1982. Blackburn shall be entitled to the Dictaphone and the Memory typewriter plus one-half of the type fonts for the memory typewriter. Marder shall be entitled to the Electronic Selectric Composer (ESC) typesetting machine, all typesetting fonts for the ESC, one-half of the typing fonts for the typewriter, the electric typewriter (currently in the possession of Blackburn), the light table, the Strip Printer, and the filing cabinet and its contents (customer files). All other miscellaneous furnishings and tools shall remain the property of Midnight Oil Typesetting.

Furthermore, Marder shall have all rights and privileges solely to the name "Midnight Oil Typesetting" and shall continue to conduct business in the usual manner under said name. All monies in the bank or owing (receivables) to Midnight Oil Typesetting shall belong to Marder and Midnight Oil Typesetting. Blackburn relinquishes any further claim to the assets of the business after April 1, 1982.

TRANSFER OF OWNERSHIP AGREEMENT
MIDNIGHT OIL TYPESETTING

PURPOSE

This Agreement between Joyce S. Marder (hereinafter MARDER) and Beverly Miller (hereinafter MILLER) shall set forth the terms and conditions by which MILLER shall purchase and take possession of the business known as Midnight Oil Typesetting (hereinafter MOT).

MIDNIGHT OIL TYPESETTING (MOT)

The business known as "Midnight Oil Typesetting" is a typesetting business consisting of certain ASSETS specified below and offering layout, paste-up and typesetting services to the general public. Joyce S. Marder is currently the sole owner of MOT and to her knowledge there are no liens against said business as of April 30, 1984. All ASSETS of the business, MOT, are owned outright by Joyce S. Marder. All regular normal and customary business expenses (rent, telephone, service contract, and answering service) due prior to May 1, 1984 shall have been paid by Marder. MOT has no current outstanding indebtedness as of April 30, 1984 to the best knowledge of MARDER.

TERMS

MILLER agrees to purchase MOT from MARDER for the sum of $15,000 to be paid as follows:

$5,000 down in the form of a certified bank check, payable the date this Agreement is signed. The balance of $10,000 to be paid in four (4) quarterly installments at 11% interest. Payments shall be made quarterly on July 31, October 31, 1984, January 31, and April 30, 1985. A Note signed by MILLER and MARDER shall be considered a part of this agreement. Said Note shall specify the terms of the above-mentioned time payments and any security agreement.

TRANSFER OF OWNERSHIP

At such time as MARDER receives the down payment of $5,000, signed copies of the Transfer of Ownership Agreement and the Note, and no sooner and no later than May 1, 1984, Title shall pass to MILLER for the ASSETS and MATERIALS specified herein (see ASSETS and MATERIALS), all legal rights to use the name "Midnight Oil Typesetting," and all rights to income generated by MOT.

ASSETS

Midnight Oil Typesetting owns the following ASSETS which shall become the property of MILLER upon fulfillment of the terms and conditions stated in this Agreement:

1 IBM Electronic Selectric Composer (ESC) Typesetting Machine
31 Typesetting Fonts for the ESC
1 Light Table
1 Blue 4-drawer Filing Cabinet and Contents
1 Typing Table
1 White Storage Cupboard
1 Kroy Type Lettering Machine
1 Agfa Stat Camera
1 Agfa Processor
1 Typing Chair
2 Green Office Chairs
1 Metal Stool
1 Blue Metal Table
1 IBM Selectric II Typewriter
5 Typing Elements
11 Fonts for Kroy Type Machine

MATERIALS

At the time of sale, the remaining inventory of the following MATERI-ALS, used in the normal conduct of business, shall be transferred to MILLER:

Operation Manual - Composer
Composer Ribbons
Kroy Ribbons
Clay Base Paper
Invoice Forms
X-acto knife, masking tape, blue pencils, glue stick, pica pole, drawing pens and ink, dictionary, CPP and CPN film and chemistry, Formatt lettering, clip board, and other such materials as are in the possession of MOT at the time of sale.

After April 30, 1984, any replacement Materials required to carry on the normal business activity of MOT, shall be the sole financial responsibility of MILLER.

GOODWILL

It is understood by both parties that there are no guarantees that the current customers which regularly or occasionally patronize MOT shall continue to do so now or anytime in the future. However, it is the intent of both parties to make an effort to maintain the customer base established by MARDER for Midnight Oil Typesetting. Therefore, MARDER agrees to do the following:

1.   TRAIN the new owner (MILLER) and her employees (Sonja and Gina Miller) in the proper use and maintenance of all equipment currently owned by MOT, for a period of one month (May), for a fee of $800. MILLER shall pay MARDER the $800 training fee in two payments due on May 15 and May 31, 1984. MARDER shall assume all legal responsibility to report and pay taxes on this income as an independent contractor (Consultant). In addition, MILLER agrees to pay MARDER a sales commission of 10% on any new work which MARDER procures for MOT after transfer of ownership.

Should the employees require further training, it shall be at the rate of $800 per month for no longer than one additional month. Thereafter, MARDER shall be free of all obligations to train the new owner and staff on a full-time basis. MARDER agrees to make herself available from time to time to offer assistance by telephone or in person at her discretion, for a period of one year from the date this Agreement takes effect.

2.   INTRODUCE the new owner to MOT's major customers, specifically, but not limited to: BALLET WEST, AMERICAN EXPRESS TRAVEL, UTAH OPERA, THE FOOD SUPPLY, X-PRESS PRINTING, SKI UTAH, COLOR 95 RADIO, CLAIR'S HALLMARK, ZEPHYR CLUB, PEWTER BY RICKER II, QUICK STOP PHOTO, JUDITH CHRISTENSEN, ZCMI MERCHANTS ASSOCIATION, WASATCH TOURING, TROPHY HUT; specifically the owner or representative of these business with whom MOT conducts business.

3.   NOTIFY in writing or by telephone the current customer list of the change of ownership; and supply MILLER with the Names, Addresses and Phone Numbers of these customers.

LICENSING AND TELEPHONE NUMBER
MARDER and MILLER shall make arrangements within one month of the date of this Agreement to have the current TELEPHONE NUMBER - 363-0447, and the REGISTRATION of the "Midnight Oil Typesetting" name transferred into MILLER's name. MILLER shall obtain any BUSINESS LICENSE(S) and SALES TAX REGISTRATION NUMBER as required by law. MILLER assumes all legal and financial responsibility for any debts incurred or accrued by MOT on or after May 1, 1984. As of April 1, 1984, MOT's normal and customary business expenses are as follows:
1.   Rent, $100/mo.
2.   Telephone, $53.37, single business line as billed.
3.   Service Contract for IBM ESC, $85.66, as billed by IBM.
4.   Answering Service, $15/month, as billed by EMC.
MARDER makes no implied or stated guarantees that the above expenses shall remain the same as stated above. MILLER understands that these expenses may increase from time to time at the sole discretion of the suppliers, and as of May 1, 1984, MILLER assumes sole responsibility for the payment of these expenses and any other services or supplies which she may procure after that date. It is MILLER's sole responsibility to pay these expenses and to terminate or maintain any agreements between MOT and its suppliers to provide these or any other services; and, generally, to handle any problems that arise.

RECORDS
All financial statements, records and receipts pertaining to MOT prior to May 1, 1984, shall remain the property of MARDER. MILLER shall have access to these records at any time, and shall be provided with copies of these documents upon request in a reasonable and timely manner.

ACCESS TO EQUIPMENT

MILLER (out of the kindness of her heart) agrees to lease the typesetting equipment to MARDER, for her personal use only (to include production of the newsletter "Delta News") in exchange for the cost of any supplies used, for a period of one year. MARDER shall make arrangements to use said equipment such that it does not interfere with the normal conduct of business of MOT in any way. After a year, MILLER may extend this arrangement at her discretion or may work out new terms and conditions with MARDER which meet their mutual desires at that time.

ACCOUNTS RECEIVABLE/BANKING

MILLER shall establish a separate checking account in her name for MOT.

All work completed by MARDER prior to May 1, 1984 shall be considered her property and, therefore, all receivables earned as of April 30, 1984, even though they may be paid on or after May 1, 1984, shall be the sole property of MARDER. All monies earned on work completed on or after May 1, 1984 shall accrue to MILLER.

SALES TAXES

MARDER shall be responsible to pay sales taxes on all money collected by her as former owner of MOT as said sales taxes become due. MILLER shall be responsible to pay sales taxes on all work completed and paid for, as of May 1, 1984.

OTHER

In the event either party shall fail to fulfill the terms of this agreement, said wronged party may seek legal redress, and if successful, shall be entitled to her costs, and a reasonable attorney's fee.

The above written terms and conditions include the entirety of the agreement between the signatories of this agreement.

5. RESOURCES

In spite of all the rules, regulations, and forms, the government really does want you to succeed. At the least, your small business will keep *you* employed and paying taxes. At best, you will employ (a lot of) other people who will also pay taxes. Here are some of the programs available through government agencies to get and keep your business going:

Small Business Administration (SBA)

Publications and Videotapes: how-to advice
504 Program: financial assistance to help small (fewer than 500 employees) businesses purchase fixed asscts that will create and retain jobs
Procurement Assistance: to help small business sell to government (get government contracts)
Advocacy: representing small business before Congress and federal agencies
Loan Programs:
    Guaranteed Business Loans
    Guaranteed Loans to Development Companies
    Bond Guarantee Program
    Physical Disaster Loans
Counseling and Training:
SCORE (Service Corps of Retired Executives): Volunteers, retired executives, provide free counseling and training to small business owners.
Small Business Development Centers (SBDCs): In partnership with state and local governments, educational institutions, and the private sector, the SBA offers training for a small fee and free consultation in business planning and bookkeeping. Consultation is provided by qualificd individuals on a one-on-one basis. Training takes the form of management courses, conferences, workshops, and seminars. SBDC also publishes newsletters.
Women's Network for Entrepreneurial Training (WNET): A mentor program. WNET pairs a five-year veteran in business with a new business owner (in business for at least one year) for a period of one year. The veteran provides consultation to achieve these goals: strengthen business skills, grow a profitable business, become a successful employer, and contribute to the economic growth of the state.

Books and Articles

The following are listed in the order in which they should be read.

Small-Time Operator: How to Start Your Own Small Business, Keep Your Books, Pay Your Taxes & Stay Out of Trouble!, by Bernard Kamorof,

C.P.A. (Bell Springs Publishing Company, 1978.)
Buy this book with mine and read it first.

Honest Business: A Superior Strategy for Starting and Managing Your Own Business, by Michael Phillips and Salli Rasberry. (San Francisco: Clear Glass Publishing Co., 1981.)
How everyone should conduct their business affairs.

The 100 Best Companies to Work for in America, by Robert Levering, Milton Moskowitz, and Michael Katz. (Addison-Wesley Publishing, Co., 1984.)
If your small business gets big, here's a good guide.

A Great Place to Work: What Makes Some Employers So Good (and Most So Bad), by Robert Levering. (New York: Avon Books, 1988.)
If the place you work now isn't "great," this book will give you the impetus to start your own.

Creating Money: Keys to Abundance, by Sanya Roman and Duane Packer. (H.J. Kramer, Inc., 1988.)
This could ease the fears you have about doing what you want, rather than working just for money.

How to Create Your Own Fad and Make a Million Dollars, by Ken Hakuta, a.k.a. Dr. Fad. (New York: Avon Books, 1990.)
Very practical advice about maintaining control over your own business, with a great resource list of distributors, toy buyers, patent organizations, and trade shows.

Women and Home-Based Work: The Unspoken Contract, by Kathleen Christensen. (Henry Holt and Company, 1988.)
A bit dated, but some good stories about the juggling act women with children face.

How to Build a Second Income Fortune in Your Spare Time, by Tyler G. Hicks. (W. Nyack, New York: Parker Publishing Company, Inc., 1965.)
Reinforces the idea that you build a business based on what you already know or do.

Working, by Studs Terkel. (New York: Avon Books, 1972.)
Invaluable insight into people and their attitudes toward work.

Age Wave: How the Most Important Trend of Our Time Will Change Your Future, by Ken Dychtwald, Ph.D. and Joe Flower. (New York: Bantam Books, 1990.)
Trends you should be aware of as an entrepreneur.

Ogilvy on Advertising, by David Ogilvy. (New York: Random House, 1985.)
The book the professionals use: first and last word on this subject.

Production for the Graphic Designer, by James Craig. (New York: Watson-Guptill Publications, 1974.)
If you need anything printed, a basic understanding of the process will save you untold amounts of grief, aggravation, and money.

127 Ways to Get More Customers, AEA Business Manual No. 973. (American Entrepreneurs Association, 1981.)
Some good examples of successful publicity efforts.

Here's my list of magazine articles that I have collected and re-read over the years for their practical advice:

"Taking the Plunge: If You're Starting a New Business, Be Prepared to Live on Your Savings," by Sanford L. Jacobs. *Wall Street Journal*, December 1, 1986.

"More than a Dream: Running Your Own Business," by Gerald Krefetz and Gittelman Film Associates. U.S Department of Labor, Employment, and Training Administration, 1981. Available from American Management Associations, 135 W 50th St., New York, NY 10020.

"Small Business," supplement to *The Wall Street Journal Reports*. Dow Jones & Company, 1988.

"Focus on the Facts." (The SBA has published a series of fact sheets in conjunction with Apple Computer, Dun & Bradstreet Information Resources, and Lotus on raising money, starting a business, planning, knowing the market, information, and cash flow.)

"How to Write Successful Classified Ads," AEA Special Report No. 994. *Entrepreneur Magazine*, 1981.

"How to Start Your Own Business," *Ms. Handbook*, by Heidi Fiske and Karen Zehring. *Ms. Magazine* Corp., 1976.

"Read This Before Starting Any Business," Entrepreneur Special Report No. 500. American Entrepreneur's Association, 1979.

"More than a Dream: Raising the Money," by Gerald Krefetz and Gittelman Film Associates. U.S. Department of Labor, 1981.

6. BUSINESS ORGANIZATIONS AND ASSOCIATIONS

Name/Address	Purpose	Member Benefits
Chamber of Commerce	Lobby state government; networking; education; advocacy.	Membership directory; associations brochure; newsletter; seminars and workshops; insurance program; business development groups.
Convention & Visitors Bureau	Convention planning & assistance; resource for related services.	List of upcoming conventions; seminars and workshops; membership directory; visitors' guide.
Better Business Bureau	Self-regulation assistance for business	Reliability reports; complaint resolution assistance, binding arbitration if necessary; consumer information; fosters ethical advertising and selling practices, monitors advertising; speakers' bureau; business advisory publications.
Travel Council branch of state government)	Promote tourism.	Publish directories of accommodations and services of interest to tourists and visitors.

Retail Merchants Association	Promote retail stores; advocacy.	Lobby local government; sponsor holiday promotions.
Women's business groups	Education; networking.	Luncheon/speaker meetings; evening socials.
Trade associations & marketing organizations	Education.	Meetings; publications.
National Association for the Self-Employed (NASE) P.O. Box 612067 DFW Airport, TX 75261-2067 (800) 232-NASE	Lobbying Congress; financial services and education for small business.	Newsletter (useful how-to information), travel, car rental, magazine discounts; business publications and tapes; consultation; credit union; computer software business systems; group insurance plan.
National Association of Private Enterprise (NAPE) P.O. Box 470397 Fort Worth, TX 76147	Discounts on business needs.	Newsletter, discounts on business machines; travel and entertainment discounts; insurance plan.
American Entrepreneurs Assoc. 3211 Pontius Avenue Los Angeles, CA 90064	Education (also publisher of *Entrepreneur Magazine*)	How-to manuals about specific types of businesses at a discount.

7. APPLICATIONS AND TAXES

Who Must Fill Out Form	Form #	FEDERAL Name of Form/Schedule	When to File or Apply/Purpose
Sole proprietor or Partner (no employees)	Form SS-5	"Social Security Number"	Apply no later than upon turning 18 years of age. Use this number when filing federal tax returns.
Partnership, Corporation, & Sole Proprietor who pays wages, pensions, or excise taxes.	Form SS-4	"Employer Identification Number (EIN)"	Apply when you open for business. Use this number when you file federal tax returns.
Your employees	Form W-4	"Employee's Withholding Certificate"	Upon being hired, and again at the end of each year if exemptions change. Used by employer to determine amount of withholding tax.
Business Owners (employers) who must withhold and pay income tax and Social Security tax FICA) for employees	Form 941, Form 8109	"Employer's Quarterly Federal Tax Deposit"	Reports (941)are due quarterly: Apr. 30, July 31, Oct. 31, Jan. 31. Actual payments of tax can be due as often as 8 times a year (8109). If deposits are made in full and on time, reporting deadline is extended 10 days.

Who	Form	Title	Description
Employers	Form W-2, Form W-3	"Wage and Tax Statement," "Reconciliation of Income Tax Withheld From Wages"	W-2 is given to all employees by Jan. 31; W-2 and W-3 are sent to Social Security Administration by last day of Feb. Records and reports wages paid and taxes withheld.
Employers	Form 940 (or 940-EZ)	"Federal Unemployment Tax (FUTA)"	Form 940 is filed 1 month after year end, by Jan. 31. Deposits are due quarterly for amounts over $100: Apr. 30, July 31, Oct. 31, Jan. 31. Unemployment insurance.
Anyone who is not self-employed (not an employee) who carries on a trade or business with the intent to make a profit	Schedule SE, Form 1040	"Social Security Self-Employment Tax"	Annual report: Apr. 15. Social Security report and Reconciliation.
Sole Proprietors	Form 1040-ES	"Tax Withholding & Estimated Tax for Individuals"	Estimated income and Social Security must be paid and reported quarterly: Apr. 15, June 15, Sep. 15, Jan. 15.
Owner of an unincorporated business —Sole Proprietors	Schedule C, Form 1040	"Profit or Loss From Business"	Annual report: Apr. 15. Used to calculate income tax (1040) and Social Security (SE) due.

Partnership	Form 1065	"U.S. Partnership Return of Income"	Annual report: Apr. 15. Reports total profit and loss of the business and total partners' income (loss).
Each Partner	Schedule K-1 Form 1065	"Partner's Share of Income, Credits, Deductions, Etc."	Annual report: Apr. 15. Shows each partner's profit or loss from the business, used to calculate income and Social Security taxes due.
All businesses	Form 4562	"Depreciation and Amortization"	File with 1040 or 1065: Apr. 15. Reports allowable business deductions on certain fixed assets.
Corporations	1120-A, 1120, 1120-S 1120-W	(the form you use will be determined by the type of corporation)	Tax returns due: Mar. 15. Estimated taxes paid periodically (1120-W).
Sole Proprietor, Partnership, Corporation, S Corporation	Form 1099	(assorted forms for assorted purposes)	Report due Jan. 31 to recipient; by Feb. 28 to IRS. Used to report payments such as dividends, interest, retirement payments, and payments to independent contractors, etc.

Who Must Fill Out Form	Name of Form	STATE Where and When to Apply or File	Purpose
Individual or Partner doing business under an assumed name	"Application to Transact Business Under an Assumed Name"	Dept. of Business Regulation or Commerce. Before you do anything else.	Registers your name and protects your right to its use where you conduct business.
Corporation	"Application for Reservation of Corporate Name"	Dept. of Business Regulation or Commerce. Before you do anything else.	Registers your corporate name.
If you sell goods or services subject to sales tax or if you employ 1 or more person(s)	"State Tax Commission Application"	State Tax Commission. Apply when you open for business.	You'll receive a Sales and Use Tax Number, and/or an Employer's Withholding Identification Number, for use when filing state tax returns.
Employer	"Quarterly Return" & "Annual Reconciliation Return"	State Tax Commission. Filed and paid quarterly, reconciled annually by Jan. 31.	Used to file and pay withholding (income) taxes.

Employer	"Status Report"	Dept. of Employment. File within 10 days of starting business.	Will determine if you must pay unemployment insurance. (Note: Unemployment insurance is supported by both federal and state taxes.)
Employer (some exceptions)		Worker's Compensation Fund, or Industrial Commission for permission to self-insure.	To provide insurance for job related injury.
Employer	"(State) Employer's Withholding Forms"	State Tax Commission. Filed quarterly or monthly; reconciled annually.	Used to file and pay state withholding (income) tax.
Corporation	"(State) Small Business Franchise Income Tax Return"	State Tax Commission. Due Apr. 15.	Corporations pay state tax based on net taxable income.

LOCAL

Who Must Fill Out Form	Name of Form	Where and When to Apply or File	Purpose
Everyone doing business	"Application for Business License"	City or county where your business will be located. Apply before or as soon as you open for business.	To obtain a business license. The process involved will ascertain whether your business and its location comply with all zoning, building, parking, health, and safety regulations.
Anyone operating a business that involves running water, food, alcohol, or adult entertainment; or if you are changing or expanding a building physically.	(Permits, licenses, and fees)	City or county where your business will be located. Local government will advise you.	When you apply for a business license, you will be told if you may need special permits or regulatory licenses, or to pay special fees.
Property owners		City or county of place of business — County Assessor. Paid annually (date varies).	Property tax is collected on building, land, and some fixed assets.

8. MISCELLANEOUS THINGS TO KNOW

Item	Resource/Contact	Publications
Determine legal structure of business	You, your partners, your accountant & attorney (if more than 2 people are involved)	SBA Pub. MP25 (formerly 6.004); IRS Pub. 334, Ch. 1.
Pick a location	Zoning & Planning Dept., Chamber of Commerce, leasing agents	SBA Pub. 2.024
Establish a record keeping system	Your accountant, you, IRS	IRS Publications: Pub. 334, Chs. 2, 3, 4; Pub. 17, Your Federal Income Tax; Pub. 463, Travel, Entertainment & Gift Expenses; Pub. 538, Accounting Periods & Methods; Pub. 556, Examination of Returns; Pub. 583, Business Record Keeping.
Buy adequate insurance	Private insurance carriers	SBA MP 28
Train your employees	You, your suppliers, private instructors, your employees	SBA Pub. PM1 (Note: Those who sell you new equipment will often provide free/low cost training.)

Item	Resource/Contact	Publications
Educate yourself	IRS, SBA, Small Business Development Centers, Banks, Consumer Information Center, universities & colleges, trade schools, community education programs, etc.	IRS publications; SBA publications; Consumer Information Center publications: P.O. Box 100, Pueblo, CO 81002
Create compensation package for employees	You, your advisors	SBA PM3
Comply with health and safety regulations	OSHA, State Industrial Commission	
Be prepared for adversity	This book, your knowledge and experience, business organizations	BBB Pub. 24-173, "Effective customer relations and complaint handling"; BBB Pub. 147, "Schemes against business"; SBA Pub. 3.008, "Outwitting Bad-Check Passers."

Index